BASIC SKILLS
Geography

Sally Naish and Katherine Goldsmith

JOHN MURRAY

Pupils' Book ISBN 0-7195-4704-0
Teachers' Resource Book ISBN 0-7195-4705-9

Other books in the Basic Skills series:

English by Paul Groves and Nigel
  Grimshaw   ISBN 0-7195-4350-9
with *Teachers' Resource Book*   ISBN 0-7195-4351-7

Arithmetic by John Deft   ISBN 0-7195-4349-5
with *Teachers' Resource Book*   ISBN 0-7195-4356-8

Science by Peter Leckstein   ISBN 0-9195-4445-9

Electronics by Tom Duncan   ISBN 0-7195-4449-1

Health, Hygiene and Safety by   ISBN 0-7195-4463-7
Di Barton and Wilf Stout

A related book on life skills:
Lifestart by John Anderson   ISBN 0-7195-4447-5

© Sally Naish and Katherine Goldsmith 1990

All rights reserved
Unauthorised duplication
contravenes applicable laws

First published in 1990
by John Murray (Publishers) Ltd
50 Albemarle Street, London W1X 4BD

Typeset by Pioneer Associates Ltd., Perthshire
Printed in England by Clays Ltd., St. Ives plc

British Library Cataloguing in Publication Data

Naish, Sally
  Basic skills geography
  Pupils' book
  1. Geography
  I. Title   II. Goldsmith, Katherine
  910

ISBN 0-7195-4704-0

CONTENTS

BRITISH ISLES SECTION 1

1	*We're off:* Regions of Britain	6
2	*What shall we do?* Capitals and countries	8
3	*Road to the Isles:* Location of Britain's islands	10
4	*Which island?* Features of Britain's islands	12
5	*On the road:* Britain's motorways	14
6	*InterCity:* Britain's rail network	16
7	*A journey in pictures:* Road signs	18
8	*Whatever the weather:* Weather symbols and forecasts	20
9	*Into hot water:* Tourist Bath	22
10	*Somewhere to stay:* Heritage York	24
11	*Finding your way:* Features of maps	26
12	*Bird's eye view:* Aerial photographs	28
13	*Shakespeare lived here:* Stratford-upon-Avon	30
14	*To the heart of England:* The National Exhibition Centre	32
15	*Inside the NEC:* Using site plans	34
16	*Diversion ahead:* Route planning	36
17	*All aboard the narrowboat:* Britain's waterways	38
18	*Seven Sisters:* A country park	40
19	*Sandcastles and sun loungers:* Planning holiday activities	42
20	*How far?* National parks	44
21	*Down the tube:* Tyne and Wear Metro & The London Underground	46
22	*All aboard for French bread:* Channel crossings	48

EUROPE SECTION 2

23	*To the land of the Vikings:* Scandinavia	50
24	*The French connection:* French railways	52
25	*Escape to the sun:* Holidays in France	54
26	*Upstream, downstream:* The Rhine waterway	56
27	*Where shall we go?* The Mediterranean	58
28	*Now for the sun:* The Spanish climate	60
29	*Sunny cities:* Weather in Europe	62
30	*Break a leg:* Ski resorts and ski reports	64
31	*Costa? Si!* Coastal Spain	66
32	*Old and new:* Spanish holidays	68
33	*All roads lead to Rome:* Main roads in Italy	70
34	*Grasping Greek graphs:* Tourism in Greece	72
35	*Away from it all:* The Greek Islands	74
36	*Eurotour:* The European Community	76

NORTH AMERICA   SECTION 3

37	*New York, New York:* Manhattan Island	78
38	*Going west:* Flying to the USA	80
39	*Crossing the continent:* Travel in the USA	82
40	*In the picture:* Tourist centres in the USA	84
41	*Hot or cold, wet or dry:* Climate in the USA	86
42	*Canada calling:* Canada	88

THE SOUTHERN CONTINENTS AND ASIA   SECTION 4

43	*Down under:* Images of Australia	90
44	*Neighbours?* Distances in Australia	92
45	*Black gold:* Oil in the Middle East	94
46	*Measuring up:* South America	96
47	*A Grand Tour:* Three weeks in South America	98
48	*Asian headlines:* Locations in Asia	100
49	*Japan by air:* Locations in Japan	102
50	*Getting around:* Tourist Tokyo	104
51	*Cairo to Casablanca:* Locations in Africa	106
52	*North and south:* Tourism in Africa	108
53	*Whose water?* African rivers	110
54	*East to west:* Time zones in the USSR	112

THE WORLD   SECTION 5

55	*Where in the world?* Continents and countries	114
56	*Full steam ahead:* World shipping	116
57	*Ports and products:* World trade	118
58	*Oil for the world:* The oil trade	120
59	*Around the world:* A world cruise	122
60	*Post early for Christmas:* Postal zones	124
61	*World Search:* A world quiz	126

ABOUT THIS BOOK

Basic Skills: Geography is divided into five sections:
1. British Isles
2. Europe
3. North America
4. The Southern Continents and Asia
5. The World

There are 61 units, each covering a different topic.

All the units include questions, but you may also see:

- 'Follow-up' boxes, e.g. **Find out...** : these are usually exercises which ask you to do some research, for example with an atlas or library books. Or you might be asked to draw a poster or plan a visit.
- *Issue!* boxes: these give you something to discuss. Your teacher may give you a **worksheet** to help you think about the issues.
- *Further Tasks...* boxes: these tell you when there is a **worksheet** with more exercises on a topic.

Your teacher will give you your own copies of crosswords and any maps which you will need to write on. Do not write in this book.

New ideas and words are printed in **bold** type. Ask your teacher to explain them to you if you are not sure what they mean.

1. BRITISH ISLES

1. WE'RE OFF:
Regions of Britain

Map **1.1** divides Great Britain into eleven **regions**. If you go on holiday, you may want to buy a map of the region you are visiting.

1 Table **1.2** shows areas where you might go on holiday. Use maps **1.1** and **1.3** to find out which regions they are in.

Copy out the table and fill in your answers. The first one has been done for you.

Area	Region
Snowdonia	6
Devon and Cornwall	
The Pennines	
Norfolk Broads	
Scottish Highlands	
Pembrokeshire coast	
Lake District	
Isle of Wight	

▲ 1.2

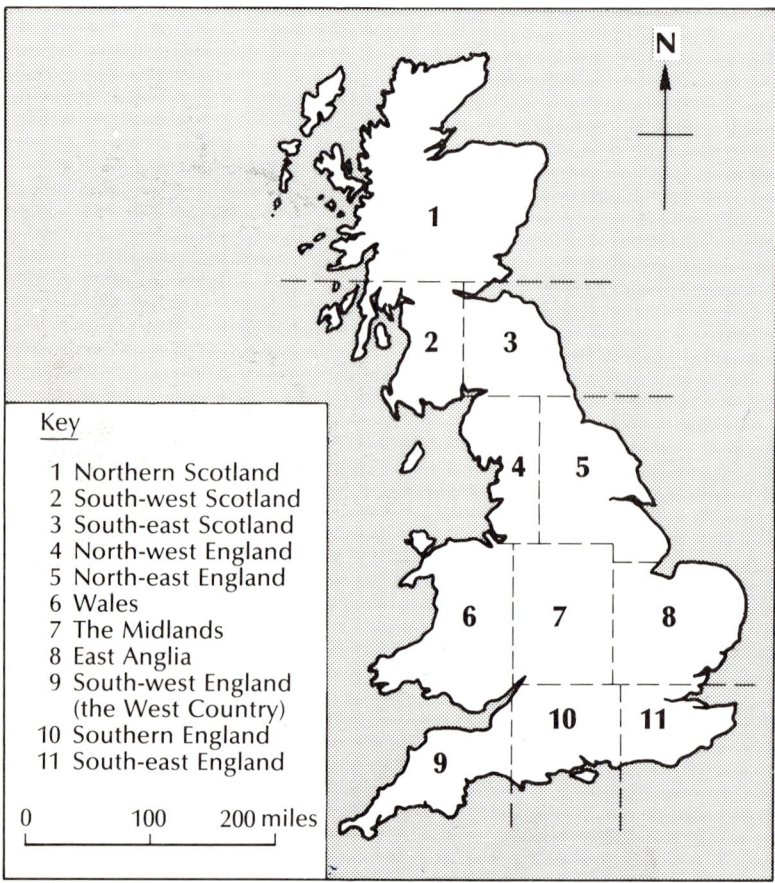

Key
1 Northern Scotland
2 South-west Scotland
3 South-east Scotland
4 North-west England
5 North-east England
6 Wales
7 The Midlands
8 East Anglia
9 South-west England (the West Country)
10 Southern England
11 South-east England

◀ 1.1 *Regions of Britain*

Instead of visiting an area you might wish to visit a particular town. You would still need a map of the region to help you find the town – or visit the countryside around it.

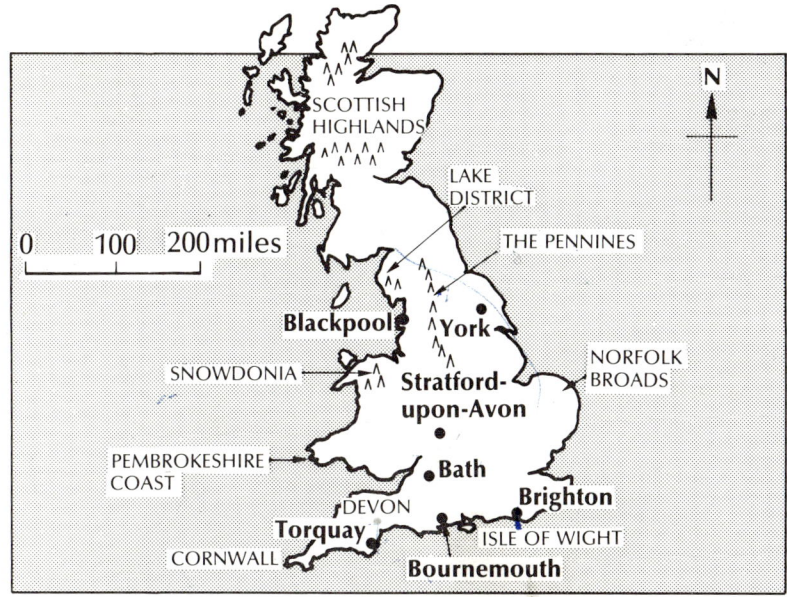

▲ 1.3 *Holiday areas and towns*

2 Copy table **1.4** and use maps **1.1** and **1.3** to fill in the number of the region each town is in. Then put a tick to show whether the town is inland or by the sea. The first one has been done for you.

Town	Region	Seaside	Inland
York	5		
Bournemouth			
Brighton			
Bath			
Torquay			
Blackpool			
Stratford-upon-Avon			

▲ 1.4

Find out . . .

Britain is divided into counties, and big cities such as London are divided into boroughs.

1. Look in an atlas to find the county or borough you live in.
2. Which counties or boroughs border it?
3. The British Isles are divided into different regions for different purposes. Find out which region you live in for electricity, water and gas supplies.

Further Tasks... More about the countries that make up the British Isles can be found on Worksheet 1.

1. BRITISH ISLES

2. WHAT SHALL WE DO?
Capitals and countries

A holiday tour operator is planning a holiday package for some American tourists. They will be in the British Isles for ten days during August.

The tourists will arrive at London Heathrow airport. They wish to visit some capital cities. They will be travelling around the British Isles by air.

1 1. Using the information on map **2.1**, copy out paragraph **2.2** filling in the missing words.

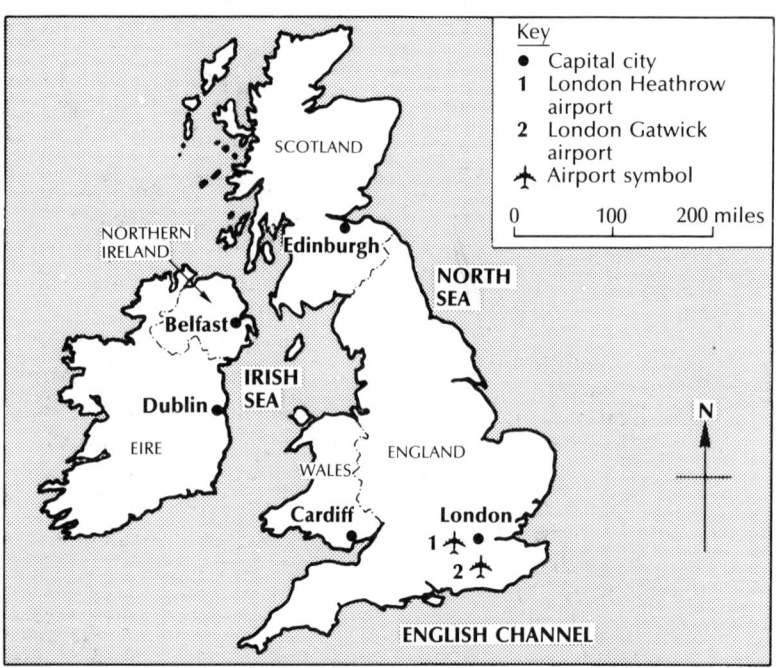

◀ 2.1 *Capitals and countries in the British Isles*

The tourists arrive at London Heathrow airport. After doing some sightseeing in London, the capital of -------, they fly north to Scotland's capital, ---------. From Scotland they go south-west to Dublin in ----.

They go on to the capital of Wales, -------, flying across the ----- Sea on the way. They return from Wales to London's second airport, -------, to catch a connecting flight to New York.

▲ 2.2

2. Which capital city did they not visit?

3. On your own copy of map **2.1** plot the route they took.

2 You have to help the tourists to plan their visit to each capital and its surrounding countryside.

Using the tourist information in extract **2.3**, advise them how to spend their time. They have three days in London, three in Edinburgh, two days in Dublin and two in Cardiff, making ten days altogether.

▼ **2.3** ▶

EDINBURGH, Scotland's beautiful capital, is surrounded by hills, woodlands and rivers. It features an extensive coastline. The ancient city is dominated by a castle, towering above gardens and excellent shops. During the summer the International Festival offers a large programme of musical and dramatic entertainment. There are museums, art galleries and the old palace of Holyrood House.

London offers an immense variety of activities: shops in Oxford Street, Carnaby Street and Knightsbridge; art galleries; museums such as the Science Museum in South Kensington; Regent's Park Zoo, Westminster Abbey, Buckingham Palace, the Tower of London. In the heart of the financial area – called the City of London – there is the tallest building in Britain, the NatWest tower. For those who want a leisurely time there are parks, boat trips on the Thames or coach trips round the city's historic sites. For evening entertainment the visitor can choose between many theatres, concert halls, night clubs, and restaurants serving food of many nationalities.

DUBLIN is a cultural centre noted for its wide streets, such as O'Connell Street, and its 18th-century squares. There is also the famous Abbey Theatre. Whiskey distilling, brewing and glassmaking are interesting industries. The countryside, especially in the nearby Wicklow Mountains, is very pleasant. The city is on the Irish Sea and is the main port of Eire.

CARDIFF is built round a Norman castle on the river Taff. Nearby are Llandaff Cathedral and the Welsh Folk Museum. The Gower Peninsula provides beautiful coastal scenery. In the Brecon Beacon mountains you can do hill walking. The Museum of Wales, Cardiff Arms Park (the home of Welsh rugby) and busy shopping areas can be found in the city.

Close to home . . .

1. Does your local area have any attractions for overseas visitors? Either draw a poster to attract visitors to your area, or find out about another tourist area and design a poster for it.

2. Which capital city do you live nearest to? Find tourist brochures about it. Use the brochures to plan a whole week's visit to the city.

1. BRITISH ISLES

3. ROAD TO THE ISLES:
Location of Britain's islands

Bird-watching, climbing, motorbike racing, French cooking, historic ruins, yacht regattas, getting away from it all: these are some of the reasons why people travel to the islands off mainland Britain.

Some of the islands, such as the Channel Islands, can be reached by air or ferry. Others, such as Anglesey, are linked to the mainland by a bridge.

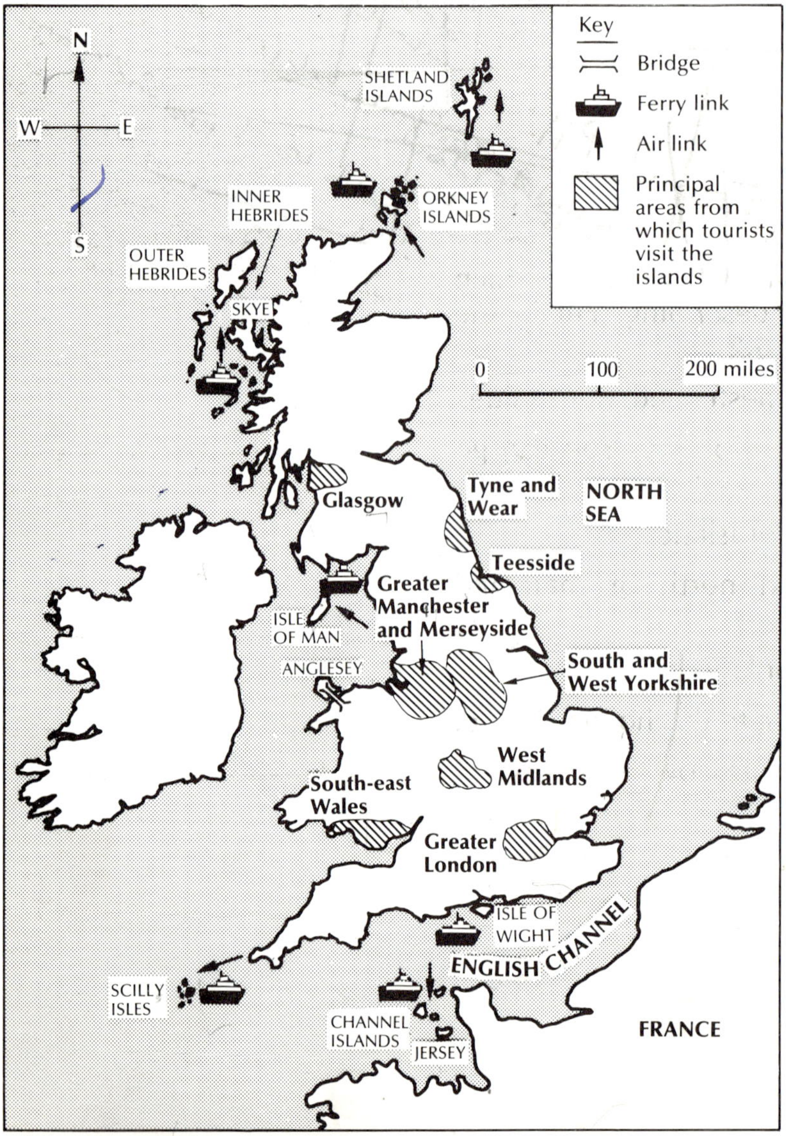

▲ *A Scottish ferry*

▲ *3.1 Islands off the coast of Britain*

▲ *The Menai Bridge, linking Anglesey to mainland Wales*

1 Using the information on map **3.1**, work out which islands these sentences are describing. Fill in the answers on your copy of grid **3.2**.

1. This island is west of Manchester and Merseyside.
2. Off the coast of the West Country. You can go there by plane or ferry.
3. The most northerly group of islands.
4. South of number 3 and north of mainland Scotland.
5. An island near the coast of France.
6. Londoners travel south-west to this holiday island.
7. This island is south of Glasgow and west of Teesside.
8. An island north-west of Glasgow.

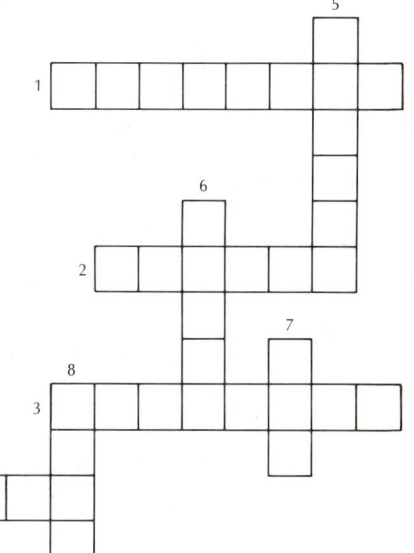

▲ 3.2

Next . . .

Using an atlas, find out the names of the islands that make up:
a) the Channel Islands
b) the Scilly Isles
c) the Outer Hebrides.

1. BRITISH ISLES

4. WHICH ISLAND?
Features of Britain's islands

1 Using map **3.1** on the previous page, the illustrations here and the following information, decide which island you would choose for a holiday. Give your reasons.

Hebrides
These are remote, wild and unspoiled islands. They are often cut off by storms in winter. The largest island is Skye, which is near to the mainland. Its highest hills are the Cuillin Hills. You can stay in one of the large villages for a climbing, fishing and sailing holiday.

Orkney and Shetland Islands
These islands were once the home of Vikings. You can still see festivals and historical sites from Viking times. The islands are of special interest because of their birds and wildlife. Recently the islands have changed because they have become a centre for North Sea oil production. There are ferry crossings from Aberdeen to Shetland and Scrabster to Orkney.

▲ *The mountains of Skye*

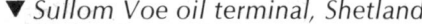
▼ *Sullom Voe oil terminal, Shetland*

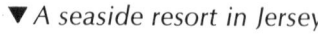
▼ *A seaside resort in Jersey*

Channel Islands
These islands are nearer to the coast of France than England. Many people who live there speak both French and English. Because taxes are very low, Channel Island towns are popular places for shopping cheaply. Some people live there to avoid taxes (**tax exiles**). The islands are reached by air, or by ferry from Weymouth or Portsmouth.

Isle of Wight

Cowes, on the Isle of Wight, is a popular yachting centre. There are other seaside resorts, such as Sandown and Shanklin, on the south-facing coast. The famous chalk **stacks**, the Needles, can be seen from the mainland. The fastest sea crossing is across the sheltered waters of Spithead, to Ryde. It takes only seven minutes by hovercraft.

Isle of Man

This peaceful island comes alive during the annual motorbike races. It is famous for the Manx cat, which has no tail. The island has mild winters because of the warm ocean current called the **North Atlantic Drift**, which flows through the Irish Sea. In the summer there are ferries from Ireland, North Wales, Merseyside and Scotland.

▲ *Yachting off the Needles, Isle of Wight*

◄ *Isle of Man TT Races*

▼ *Daffodils in the Scilly Isles*

Scilly Isles

The Scilly Isles are made up of several small islands, such as St Mary's and Tresco, with rocky coasts and sandy bays. Like the Isle of Man, they are mild in winter because of the North Atlantic Drift. They are important for growing early flowers, especially daffodils.

Both the Orkney Islands and the Shetland Islands have recently become centres for North Sea oil production. This has changed life for many of the islanders. For example, in the past, young people used to move away as there were few jobs available on the islands.

On the other hand, the oil developments have led to problems on the islands. Worksheet 4 explores this issue.

1. BRITISH ISLES

5. ON THE ROAD:
Britain's motorways

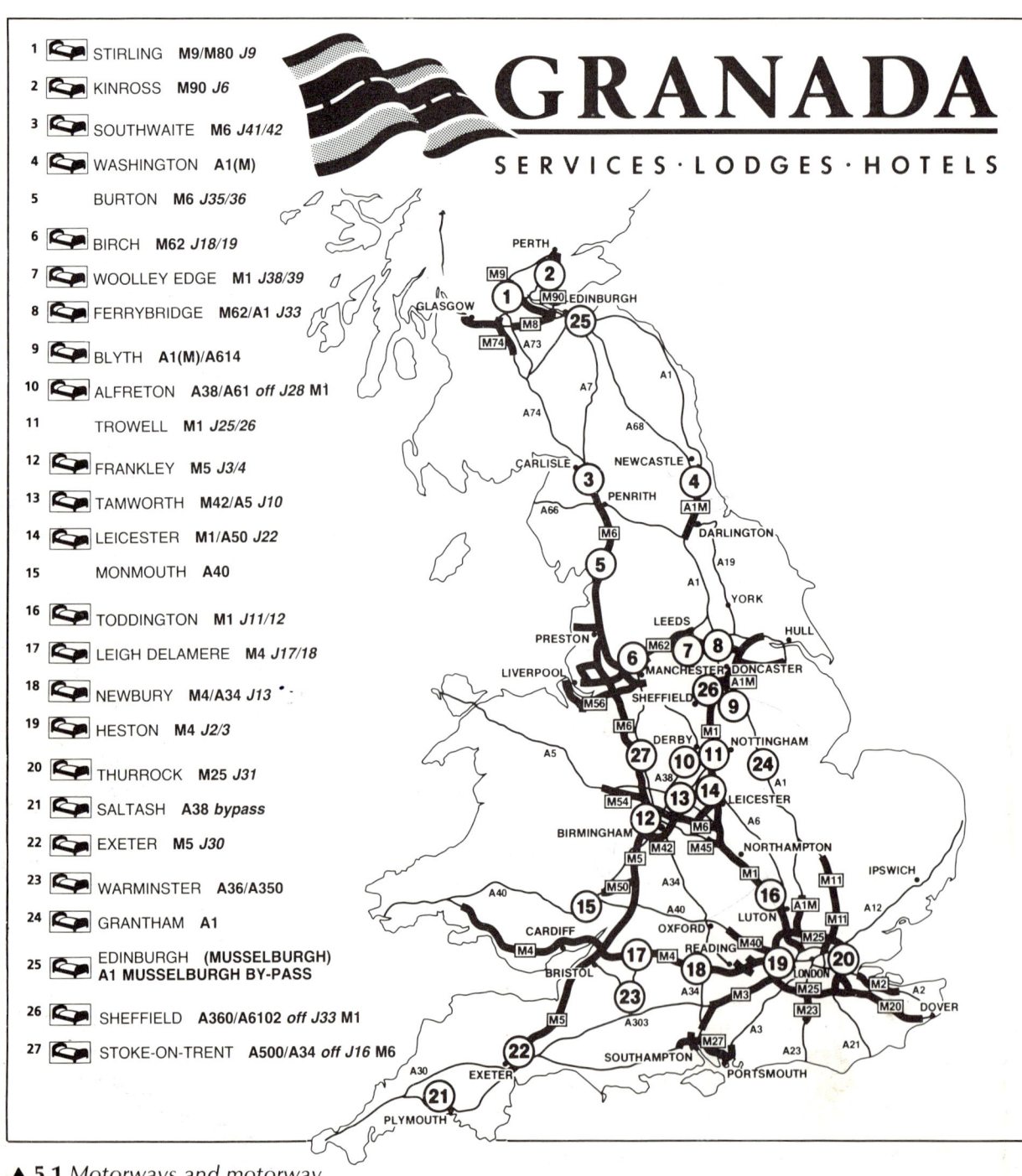

1 STIRLING M9/M80 J9
2 KINROSS M90 J6
3 SOUTHWAITE M6 J41/42
4 WASHINGTON A1(M)
5 BURTON M6 J35/36
6 BIRCH M62 J18/19
7 WOOLLEY EDGE M1 J38/39
8 FERRYBRIDGE M62/A1 J33
9 BLYTH A1(M)/A614
10 ALFRETON A38/A61 off J28 M1
11 TROWELL M1 J25/26
12 FRANKLEY M5 J3/4
13 TAMWORTH M42/A5 J10
14 LEICESTER M1/A50 J22
15 MONMOUTH A40
16 TODDINGTON M1 J11/12
17 LEIGH DELAMERE M4 J17/18
18 NEWBURY M4/A34 J13
19 HESTON M4 J2/3
20 THURROCK M25 J31
21 SALTASH A38 bypass
22 EXETER M5 J30
23 WARMINSTER A36/A350
24 GRANTHAM A1
25 EDINBURGH (MUSSELBURGH) A1 MUSSELBURGH BY-PASS
26 SHEFFIELD A360/A6102 off J33 M1
27 STOKE-ON-TRENT A500/A34 off J16 M6

GRANADA
SERVICES · LODGES · HOTELS

▲ 5.1 *Motorways and motorway service stations*

14

Motorways are linked to each other and to **A roads** to form a network. Map **5.1** shows this network.

Sometimes drivers have a choice of route. They can travel on A roads (many of which are dual carriageways) or on motorways. Motorways tend to be faster because they have fewer junctions.

The map also shows Granada service stations. A lorry driver travelling from Reading to Cardiff could get a bed for the night at Leigh Delamere. How can you tell this?

Some people think that motorways spoil the countryside. Others believe that motorways are necessary to take traffic away from towns and allow quick travel from place to place. What do you think?

Issue!

1
1. Look at map **5.1**. If you were picking up a friend at Heston service station and travelling to Exeter, you would have a choice of routes. One choice would be: Heston – M25 – M3 – A303 – Exeter. What other route could you take?

2. Now work out two different routes from London to Doncaster.

3. Why do drivers sometimes choose a non-motorway route?

2 Look at the five signs in diagram **5.2**. They all show the starting point and finishing point of a motorway journey, and a service station where a driver might want to stop on the way. Using map **5.1**, fill in on your own copy of the diagram the number of the motorway (M) and the junction number (J) where the driver would have to turn off for the service station shown. The first is done for you.

More . . .

There are many excellent motorways in European countries. Find out what motorways are called in France, Germany and Italy. What European motorways will be linked to Britain by the Channel Tunnel?

An atlas map or a road map of the European countries will help you with this.

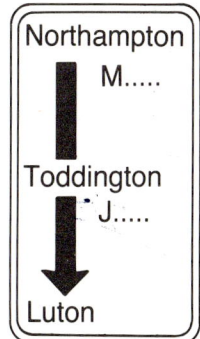

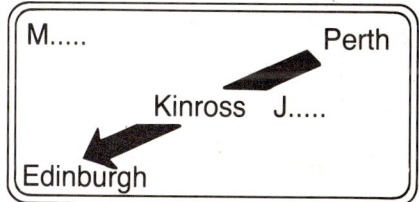

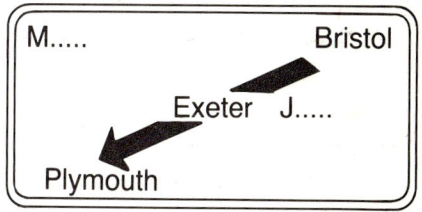

▲ 5.2

1. BRITISH ISLES

6. INTERCITY:
Britain's rail network

Map **6.1** shows the main railway routes in Britain. The rail network links the biggest cities and towns to one another.

It also links the cities to the main airports and docks. How can you tell this from the map?

The InterCity network can be a very fast way to travel around Britain. Table **6.2** shows some expected journey times from London.

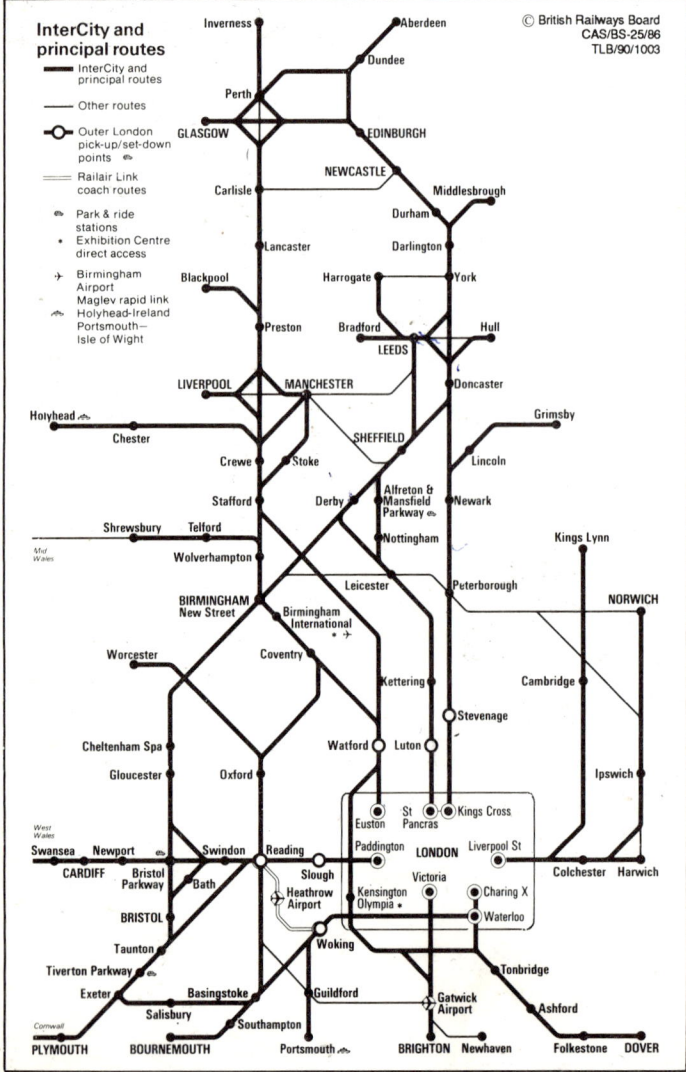

London to:	Journey time
Brighton	under 1 hour
Exeter	2 hours
Newcastle	3 hours
Norwich	2 hours
Inverness	8–11 hours
Glasgow	5½ hours
Cardiff	2 hours
Southampton	just over 1 hour
Liverpool	2½ hours
Sheffield	2½ hours
Milton Keynes	under 1 hour

▲ 6.2

◀ 6.1 The InterCity rail network

1

1. You are a travel agent. You have to advise some clients on how to get from London to their destination. Copy out table **6.3**. Use map **6.1** and table **6.2** to work out which London station they would need to set out from and how long their journey might take them.

2. If your clients were travelling from London to Leeds there are two possible routes they could take. Make a list of the stations they would go through travelling from London St Pancras to Leeds, and from London King's Cross to Leeds.

2 Table **6.4** shows a simplified extract from a British Rail timetable for trains from London to Stafford (in the Midlands). The timetable uses symbols. Using the key to the symbols say whether the following statements are true or false.

1. Passengers can catch the 17.55 train on a Saturday.
2. Passengers can get a meal on the 11.30 train on a Tuesday.
3. Passengers are advised to make a seat reservation on the 16.00 train on a Sunday.
4. The cheap ticket called a 'Saver' is not valid on the 17.05 train.

Destination	London station	Likely journey time
Sheffield		
Norwich		
Brighton		
Cardiff		
Liverpool		
Inverness		

▲ 6.3

INTERCITY
London → Stafford
Principal train service 2 October 1989 to 13 May 1990

Mondays to Saturdays			Sundays		
	London Euston depart	Stafford arrive		London Euston depart	Stafford arrive
	0635	0818		0810	1014
✕	0820	1003		0810	1018
✕	0920 sx	1056		0810	1034
	0920 so	1056		0930	1136
✕	1050	1225		0930	1149
✕	1130	1304		1050	1256
✕	1350	1520		1050	1317
	1505	1644		1330	1539
R	1600 sx	1734		1330	1543
	1600 so	1734		1330	1551
P	1650 sx	1824	R	1530	1723
	1650 so	1824	R	1600	1743
■✕	1705	1846	R	1650	1828
R	1720 fo	1857	R	1705	1855
	1733	1920	R	1735	1913
R	1755 sxp	1929	R	1850	2033
✕	1850	2028	R	1910	2137
	1900 so	2034		2020	2202
	2020 sx	2159	R	2200	2345
	2030 so	2205	R	2320	0100
R	2145 so	2326		2359	0151
R	2145 so	2344			
R	2200 sx	2342			
	2320 sx	0058			
	2320 so	0123			
	2320 so	0136			
	2359 sx	0148			
	2359 so	0206			
	2359 so	0218			

Notes
so Saturdays only
sx Saturdays excepted
✕ Service of meals including hot food to customers travelling First Class (and Standard, provided accommodation is available) on Mondays to Fridays
R Train on which reservation is advisable
R Reserved seats, which are issued free of charge to holders of valid tickets, are essential for all or part of the journey
■ SAVERS are NOT valid on this train Mondays to Fridays

▲ 6.4

Find out ...

The journey time between Edinburgh and London has decreased over the last eighty years from 9½ hours to 4½ hours. Look in library books to find out why rail travel has got faster.

Rail travel between cities is usually faster than travelling by car. Make a list of other advantages of rail travel over road travel.

1. BRITISH ISLES

7. A JOURNEY IN PICTURES:
Road signs

1 Here is a description of a day in the country. Work out what the symbols mean and rewrite the story. You can check the symbols in the Highway Code.

Andrew and Alison Simpson live in Southampton. They decided to go for a day out in the New Forest by car.

On the main road to Hythe the traffic slowed down because an electricity cable was being laid and there were [roadworks]. They were diverted through Marchwood. Soon the New Forest was in view and a few minutes later they turned left over a cattle grid into the forest. They were aware of the hazards of [deer] and [wild horses] crossing the road so they drove carefully to the National Motor Museum at Beaulieu.

Later, on the way to Brockenhurst, they passed under a railway bridge where a sign showed [14'6"]. A few minutes later they had to stop at a [level crossing] at the top of Brockenhurst High Street. Once through the High Street and across the  they headed for Lyndhurst. The traffic was busy there and everyone had to follow a  system.

At Fordingbridge, the Simpsons had a cream tea. There were many holiday-makers in the area and Alison commented on the yellow HR signs and signs directing people to a  .

Apart from having to wait for five minutes where a lane crossed a main road with the sign , there were no more delays and by driving carefully where they saw , the Simpsons arrived home safely.

2 What are the dangers here?

Make up your own story . . .

Only a few of the Highway Code symbols are used here. Write your own story about a journey in your local area, using other Highway Code symbols. You could also make up an imaginary journey.

Further Tasks... on map symbols can be found on Worksheet 7.

1. BRITISH ISLES

8. WHATEVER THE WEATHER:
Weather symbols and forecasts

Symbols are used in the newspapers and on television to describe the weather.

This ☀ shows sunshine.

This ☁ shows cloud and this 🌧 cloud and rain.

What do you think this ⛅ shows?

There are also symbols for lightning ⚡ and snow ❄.

This ⑮ indicates the temperature in degrees centigrade.

Arrows show wind direction. The wind takes its name from the direction it comes from.

This ↓ is a north wind and this ← is an east wind. Arrows with numbers ⑩↙ show the direction of the wind and its speed in miles per hour.

1. 1. Look at map **8.1**. Write a sentence to describe the weather conditions found over Ireland, northern Scotland and eastern England.
   2. What is the wind direction off the coast of south-east England?
   3. What is the wind direction off the coast of north-west Scotland?
   4. What time of year do you think the map is showing? Why?

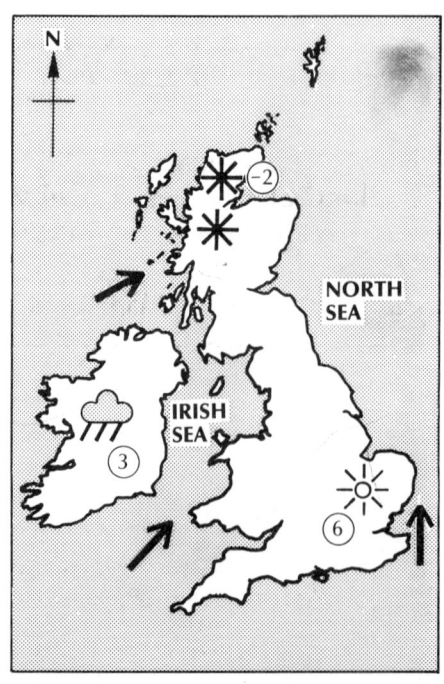

▲ 8.1 *Weather conditions in Britain*

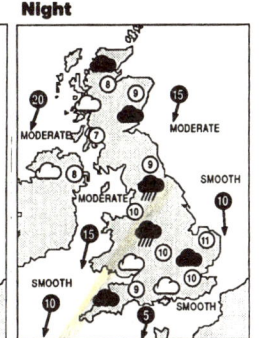

▲ 8.2 *Weather forecast, 8 June*

2 Map **8.2** shows a weather forecast for 8 June. The word 'smooth' means that the sea is calm, whereas 'moderate' means it is slightly rough.

1. Why would it be better to cross the North Sea in the evening and the Irish Sea in the morning of this day? (Map **8.1** shows where these two seas are.)
2. In which part of Britain was the best weather forecast?

In Britain we usually have **equable** (not extreme) weather with reliable rainfall, but sometimes we have unexpected weather conditions.

In 1976 and again in 1989 there was a **drought** in England and Wales. A dry winter was followed by a hot summer with low rainfall. Do you know how the Water Authorities tried to deal with these and other water shortages? Worksheet 8 will help you.

Find out . . .

More about unexpected weather conditions in Britain.

1. Ask an older person what was unusual about the winter of 1962–3.
2. From Geography or library books find out what happened in Lynmouth in August 1952.
3. Can you remember what happened in south-east England on 16 October 1987?

1. BRITISH ISLES

9. INTO HOT WATER:
Tourist Bath

Map **9.1** shows the centre of Bath. It is famous for its Roman baths and hot springs.

▼ *9.1 Street plan of Bath*

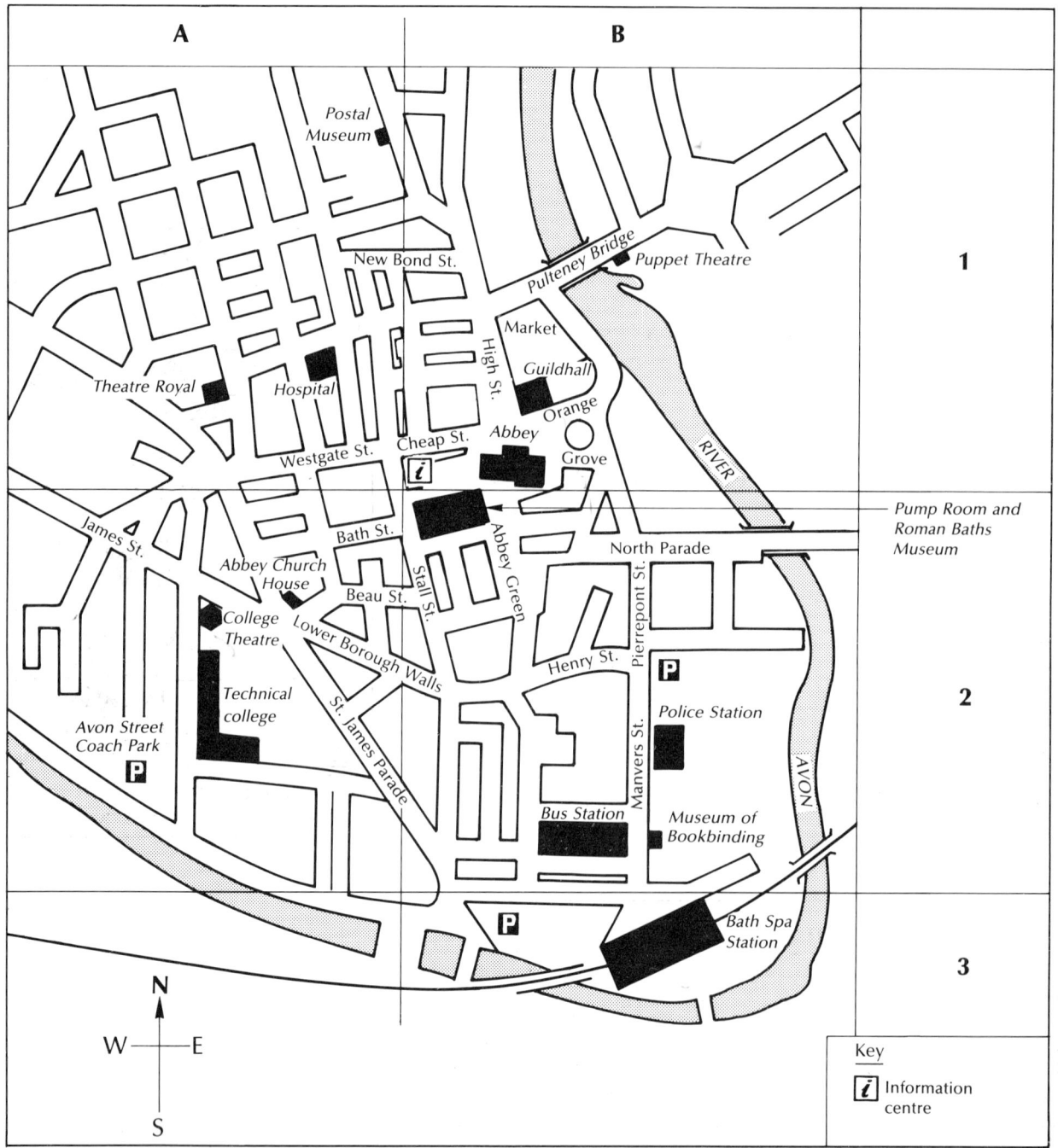

1
1. Name the street where you can find all the following: The Museum of Bookbinding, the Bus Station and the Police Station.
2. In what direction would you walk from the Puppet Theatre to the Tourist Information Office in Cheap Street?
3. What is the name of the river which goes under Pulteney Bridge?

The map has been drawn on a grid and the squares are numbered and lettered.

Two visitors travelling by train would arrive at Bath Spa station in square B3. Map **9.2** is a sketch-map showing their route from the station to the High Street in square B1. Note that the simple sketch-map is not drawn to scale and leaves out details that are not needed. Street names are added, and any landmarks that the visitor would be likely to notice.

▼ 9.2

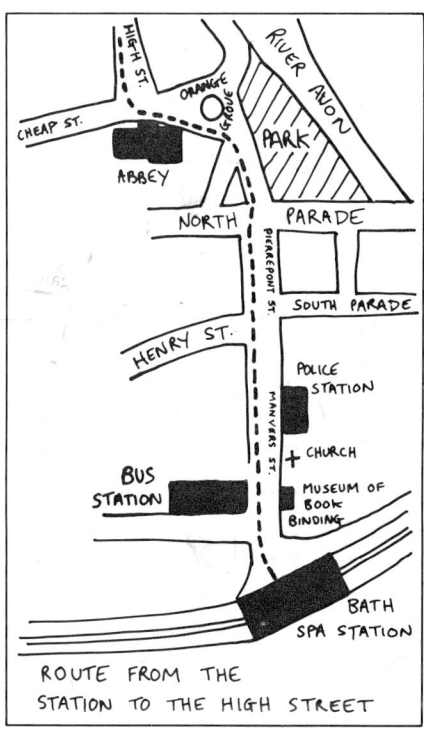

ROUTE FROM THE STATION TO THE HIGH STREET

2
1. Draw your own sketch-map to show the route from the coach park in Avon Street (square A2) to the Pump Room and Roman Baths Museum in square B2. Mark any landmarks along the way.
2. Copy and complete table **9.3**.

Feature	Square
Information Centre	
Theatre Royal	
Technical College	
Postal Museum	
Guildhall	
Abbey Church House	

▲ 9.3

Find the connection . . .

There are many other historic tourist centres in the United Kingdom. Try to find out, using books in the library, what the following places have in common: Gloucester, Durham, Norwich, Exeter, Canterbury, Chester.

1. BRITISH ISLES

10. SOMEWHERE TO STAY:
Heritage York

York is a very busy **heritage town**. People from Britain and overseas visit the ancient walled city to see places such as York Minster, the Jorvik Viking Museum and the medieval buildings of the 'Shambles'.

The city has accommodation to suit many different types of visitors, from wealthy tourists to school parties.

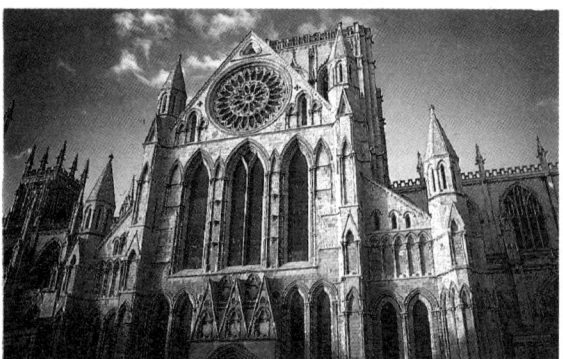

◀ *York Minster*

The Shambles ▶

1 Diagram **10.1** is the framework for a bar graph to show how many there are of each type of place to stay. The first two bars have been filled in. Copy diagram **10.1** and fill in the rest using the information in box **10.2**. You'll find it easiest if you use graph paper.

- 2 inns with accommodation
- 5 youth hostels or residential study centres
- 50 bed and breakfast establishments
- 86 small hotels and guest houses
- 44 large hotels

▲ **10.2**

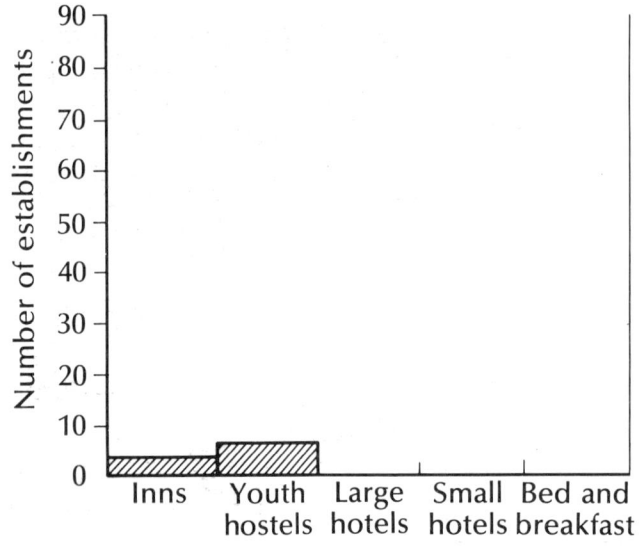

◀ **10.1**

24

2 Table **10.3** is a section of York's official list of hotels and guest houses. The abbreviations are explained in the key.

1. Which hotel would you choose if you wanted to stay in York at Christmas time?
2. Where could you have lunch?
3. Private parking is useful in a busy city. Which hotels have this?
4. Which from this list would offer all these things?

▼ 10.3

		Key	
Anker Guest House	C L TV SD T/C OS * CM		
Annjoa House	C L TV PTV B BS SD T/C OS GV(10–14) *	C	Special terms for children
Arndale Hotel	C L PTV P B BS T/C OS GF * D	L	Lounge for daytime use
Arnot House	C L PTV P SD T/C OS GF * CM	TV	Communal television
		PTV	Some rooms with private television
Ashbourne Hotel	C L TV P BS SD OS ■ *	P	Private parking
Avimore House Hotel	C L TV PTV P BS SD T/C OS GF ■ * CM GV(10–20)	B	Cots available
		BS	Baby sitting service
Bank House	C L TV PTV BS SD T/C * GV(16)	SD	Special diets on request
Barbican Hotel	C L TV PTV B BS SD T/C * GV(16)	T/C	Tea/coffee making facilities
Barclay Lodge	C L TV PTV P B BS SD OS ■ * CM GV(10–20)	OS	Off season bargain breaks
		GF	Some rooms on ground floor
Barrington House	C PTV T/C OS D *	■	Lunch served by request
Bedford Hotel	C L TV PTV B SD T/C OS D ■ * CM GV(10)	*	Dinner by request
		CM	Open at Christmas
		D	Dogs by arrangement
		GV	Group visits by arrangement. The number in brackets indicates the maximum number.

What would you think . . . ?

Cities like York, Bath, Edinburgh and other heritage towns have many attractions for tourists. On the other hand, tourism brings advantages and disadvantages for the local people. For example, traffic can be very bad in York.
What would you think about tourists if you were one of the following and lived in a tourist centre?
a) a mother with young children
b) the owner of a café
c) a local shopkeeper
d) a hotel manager
e) a disabled person
f) a teenager

1. BRITISH ISLES

11. FINDING YOUR WAY:
Features of maps

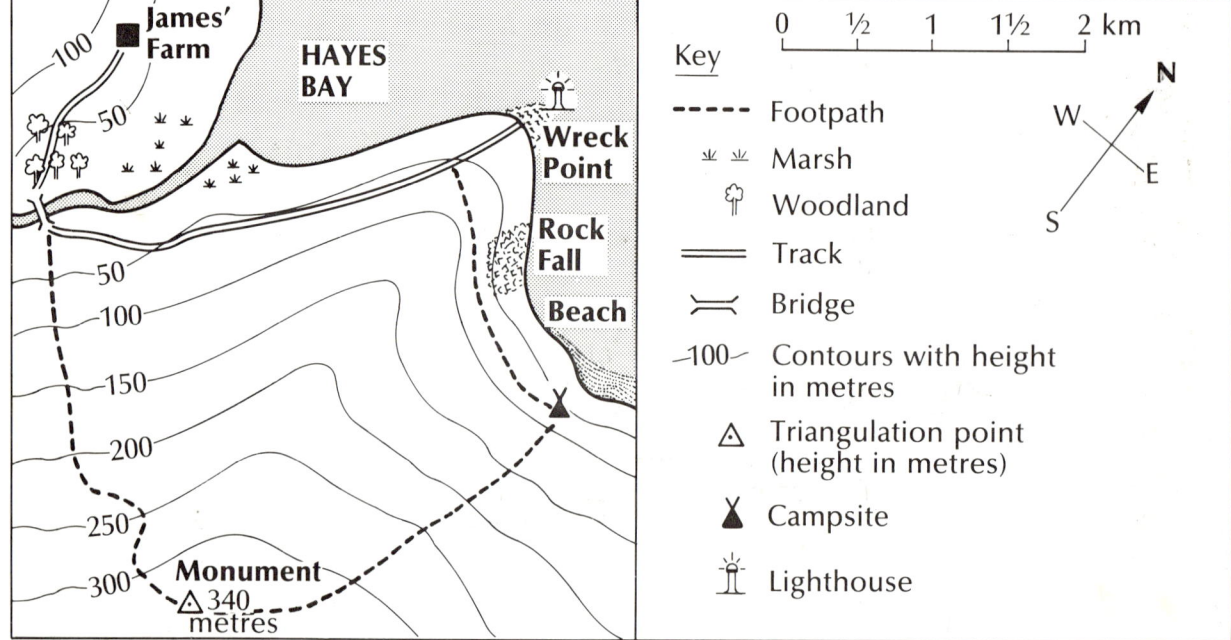

▲ 11.1

Every map should have a title indicating what the map is about, a scale, points of the compass, symbols and a key.

A title
The title is missing on map **11.1**. The following titles have been suggested for it:
a) The coastline near Hayes Bay
b) Footpaths to Monument Hill
c) A coastal area
Which do you think is the most helpful?

A scale
The scale helps you to work out actual distances between places. You can put your ruler on the scale and work out how many centimetres on the map represent one kilometre on the ground. What is the scale used in map **11.1**?

Points of the compass
These show direction. North has been at the top of the maps you have used so far in this book, but this is not always the case, as you can see in map **11.1**.

Symbols

Symbols are signs on a map used to show things that you would find in the area. They save space and can be easily spotted.

1 The map contains a lot of information about the way the land is used, the coastline and the height of the land.

1. Write four sentences about the coastline using the information on the map.
2. Why does the track from the farm to the lighthouse take a roundabout route?

Contour lines join up places which are at the same height. Sometimes particular heights, especially at the top of hills, are shown by **spot heights** or **triangulation points**. There is a triangulation point at the Monument on this map. The height of the land at James' farm is 75 metres above sea level. The camp site is 50 metres above sea level, so James' farm is 25 metres higher than the camp site.

2
1. How much higher is the Monument than a) the camp site; b) the farm?
2. What direction is the campsite from the Monument?
3. What direction is the Monument from the farm?
4. How far is it in a straight line from James' Farm to the Monument? Use your ruler and the scale to work it out.
5. If you lay a piece of string on the track, you can work out the distance you would walk between two places. How far would you have to walk to get from James' Farm to the Monument?

Next step . . .

Using an Ordnance Survey map of countryside near to where you live, plan a walk of about 12 kilometres. Try to avoid walking on roads all the time, but make sure you are near a village where you could buy a drink at lunchtime. Using the map describe what you would see on your walk.

Further Tasks... on country walks can be found on Worksheet 11.

1. BRITISH ISLES

12. BIRD'S EYE VIEW:
Aerial photographs

Photo **12.1** is a recent aerial photograph of part of Reading. Map **12.2** is an earlier map of the same area.

© CROWN COPYRIGHT

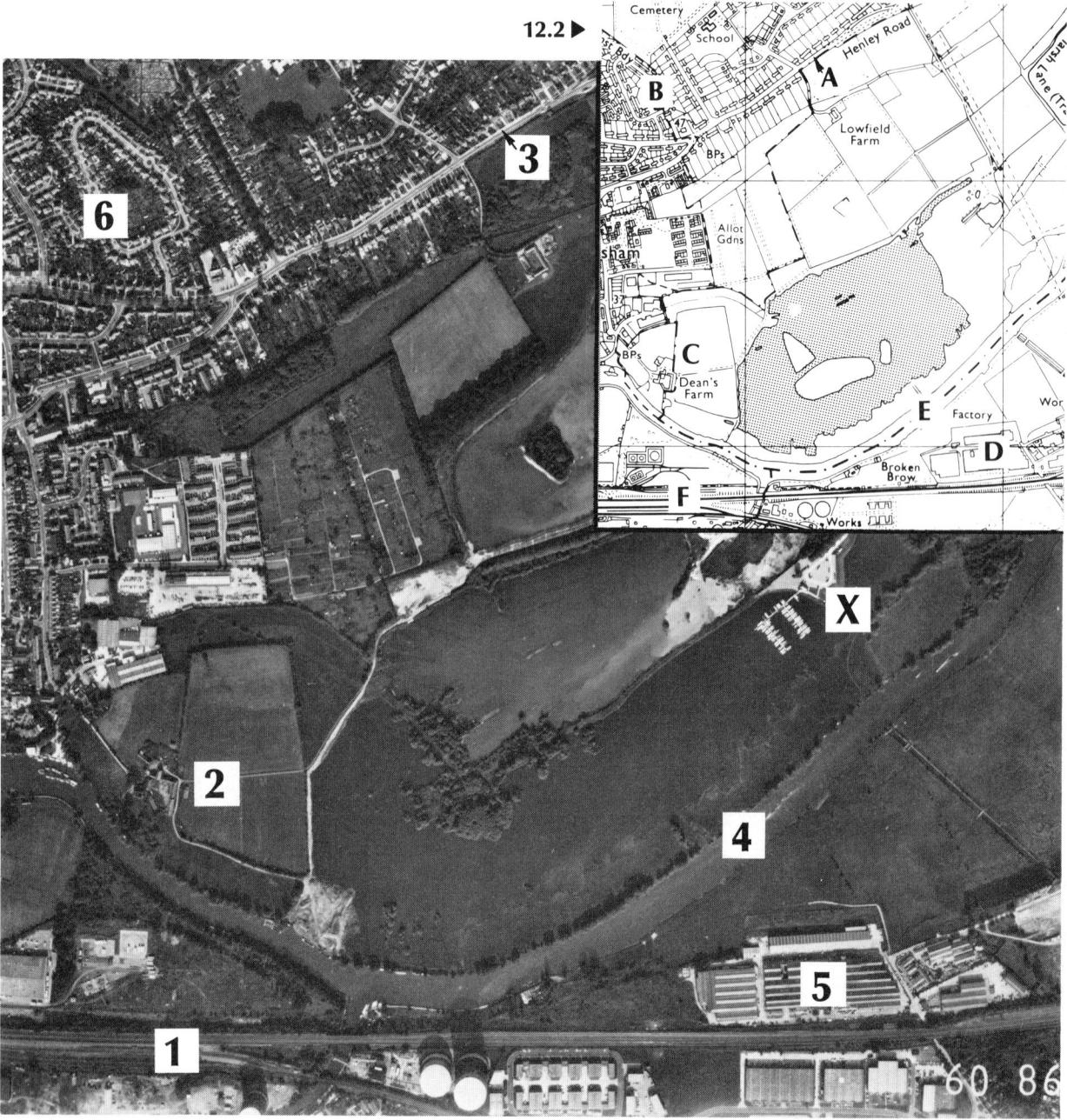

▲ 12.1

1 Copy out table **12.3**. Match up the features marked 1–6 on photo **12.1** with the corresponding features marked A–F on map **12.2**. Write the correct letter in the second column. In the third column write a description of each feature.

2 Can you see any changes that took place between the time when the map was drawn and the time when the photo was taken?

Photo 12.1	Map 12.2	Description
1		
2		
3		
4		
5		
6		

▲ 12.3

Reading is a fast growing town 40 miles from London. Because it is close to London, Heathrow airport and the M4, it has become a favourite place for High Tech and computer companies to base themselves. It has very low unemployment.

On the other hand, because it is a fast growing town, the surrounding countryside is under pressure. Companies want more land to build their factories on. People want more land to build their houses on.

The area shown in the photo is going to be developed for industry and for housing.

3 1. Whereabouts in this area do you think it would be possible to build some new houses?

2. Think of two reasons why this might be a nice place to live.

The lakes shown on the map were created by the flooding of gravel pits. When the pits were being dug, people probably thought they were very ugly. Now they provide an area for people to sail, fish and walk. On the photo, X marks a new mooring for sailing boats.

Many towns are now trying to turn old industrial areas into land for recreation. Is there a development like this in your area? Worksheet 12 examines how you might find this out.

1. BRITISH ISLES

13. SHAKESPEARE LIVED HERE:
Stratford-upon-Avon

Stratford-upon-Avon was the home of William Shakespeare, Britain's most famous playwright. More than half a million people visit his birthplace every year – many of them overseas tourists – making it one of Britain's most popular historical sites.

Stratford also has the Royal Shakespeare Theatre where the Royal Shakespeare Company performs. People who live within easy travelling distance can visit the theatre for the evening.

Table **13.1** gives information about the major towns and cities near Stratford.

Town	Distance from Stratford	Population in 1981
Banbury	20 miles	35,796
Birmingham	24 miles	920,389
Coventry	19 miles	314,124
Gloucester	39 miles	92,200
Oxford	40 miles	98,521
Worcester	24 miles	74,247

▲ 13.1

1 Using the information in table **13.1**, which town would you expect to provide most evening visitors for Stratford and which the least? Give your reasons.

2 An American family – the Carters – have asked you to help them plan their day trip to Stratford. They want to visit as many of the Shakespeare tourist attractions as possible. The itinerary (journey plan) they have been given by their American travel agent is shown in **13.2**.

Park in the car park by Bridgefoot. I suggest you then take in the audiovisual show at the World of Shakespeare. The show is only 25 minutes long.

I've booked you a back-stage tour at the Royal Shakespeare Theatre at 11.15 a.m. - don't be late or they won't let you in.

Shakespeare's birthplace is the next stop. You can also get lunch right next door.

If it's a fine day, walk (one mile) across the fields (the footpath is well marked) to Anne Hathaway's cottage. She was Shakespeare's wife. It's a <u>very</u> English cottage.

You'll have time for a cream tea on the way back, then you must visit Holy Trinity Church, where Shakespeare is buried. It's right next to the river.

Your show - 'Macbeth' at the Royal Shakespeare Theatre - is at 7.00 p.m. Don't be late!

1. Make your own copy of sketch-map **13.3**. Using the key, draw in the route that the Carters are going to take.
2. Which Shakespeare tourist attraction will they not visit?
3. They may come to Stratford by train instead of by car. Suggest a better order for them to visit the same tourist attractions, starting at the station.

▲ 13.2
▼ 13.3

key
1. Royal Shakespeare Theatre
2. Shakespeare centre and Shakespeare's birthplace
3. Holy Trinity Church - Shakespeare's Tomb
4. World of Shakespeare - audiovisual presentation
5. Anne Hathaway's cottage
6. New Place - where Shakespeare died

0   ¼   ½ Mile

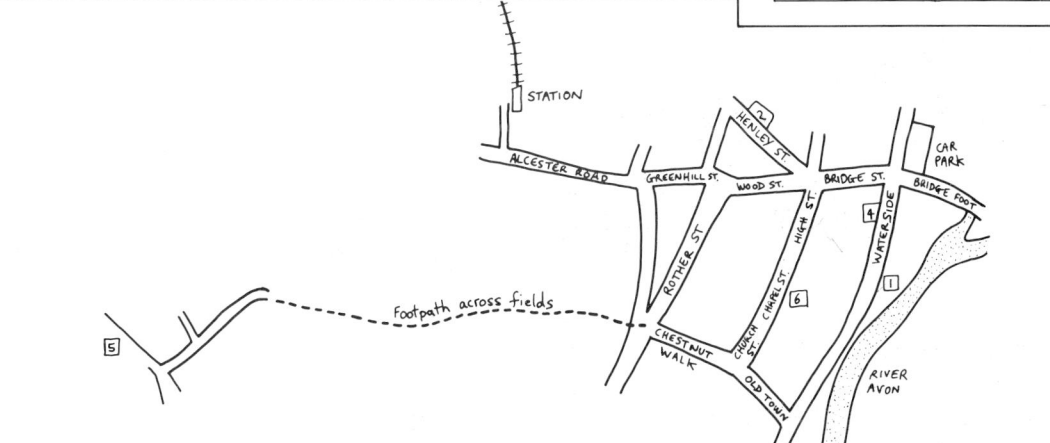

STRATFORD - UPON - AVON

31

1. BRITISH ISLES

14. TO THE HEART OF ENGLAND:
The National Exhibition Centre

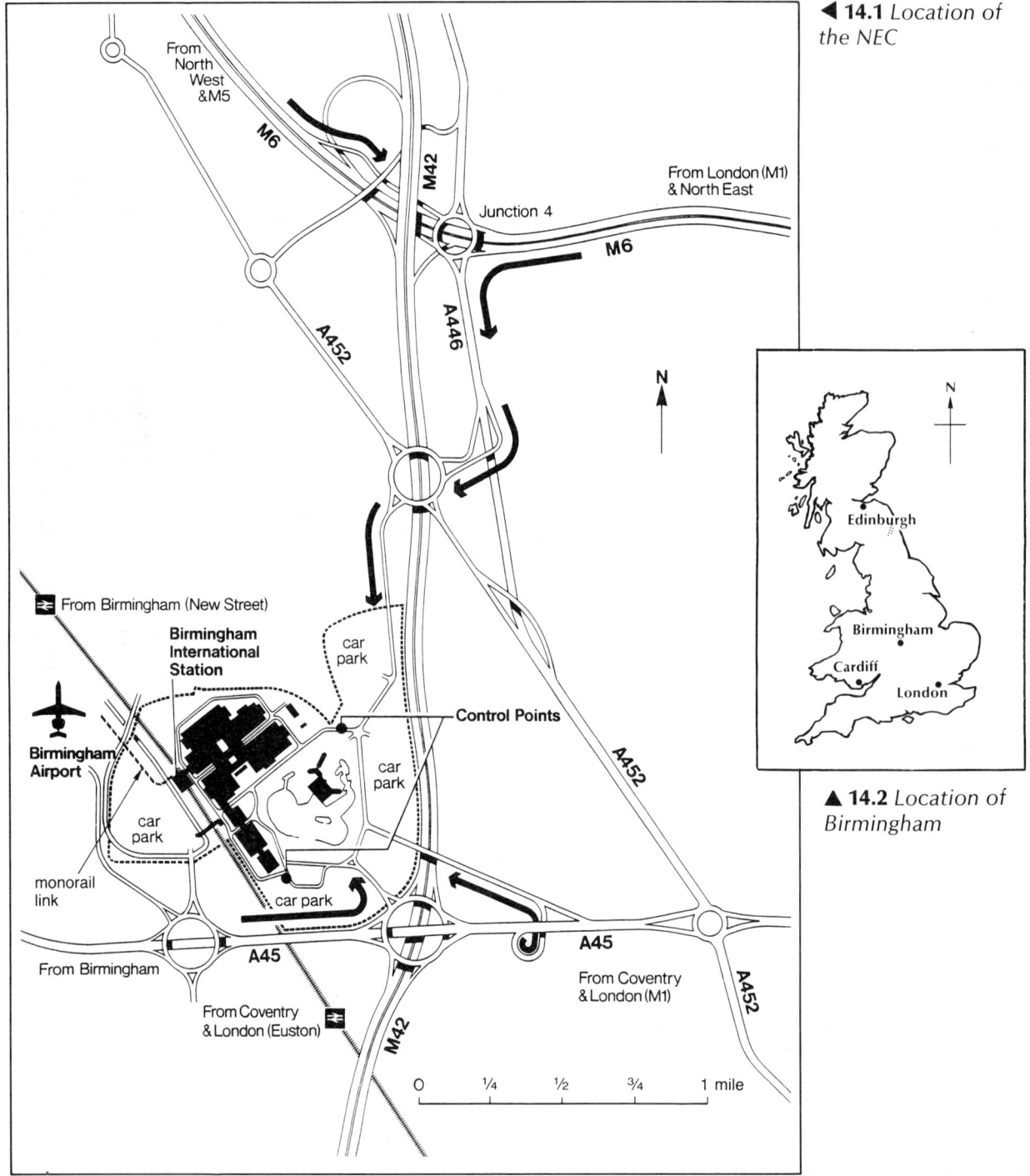

◄ 14.1 *Location of the NEC*

▲ 14.2 *Location of Birmingham*

The National Exhibition Centre (NEC) in Birmingham is a huge complex where exhibitions, concerts, festivals, conferences and indoor and outdoor sporting events take place.

The Exhibition Centre lies to the south-east of Birmingham. Maps **14.1** and **14.2** show that the NEC is right in the heart of the country. It is very **accessible** (easy to get to). Visitors who arrive by air at Birmingham International airport have only a 90 second monorail ride to the NEC.

Birmingham International railway station, marked on map **14.1**, is 10 minutes from Birmingham New Street station, which is 80 minutes from London Euston. The M6 is very near, as can be seen on map **14.1**. It links the Centre to the M1, M5, M42 and M40.

There is parking for 1500 vehicles. Shuttle buses take the public from the car parks to the buildings.

1 Copy out the paragraph below, and using maps **14.1** and **14.2** fill in the missing words.

The hot favourites for the basketball championship, from Carlisle in north-west England, arrive by the M____. They come off the motorway at junction ____ and take the A____ to the Exhibition Centre. The challengers, travelling from London up the M____, take a break in Coventry before continuing along the A____ and A____ to the Centre.

Getting there . . .

1. Use a road atlas showing main roads and motorways to find out which roads visitors to the NEC could take from the following towns and cities: Dundee, Cambridge, Derby, Ipswich, Leicester, Middlesbrough, Stoke-on-Trent, Swansea, Swindon.

2. Use an atlas to find out which of the following airports would be next nearest to the NEC if Birmingham International airport was closed by fog:
   a) Manchester
   b) Stansted
   c) Heathrow.

1. BRITISH ISLES

15. INSIDE THE NEC:
Using site plans

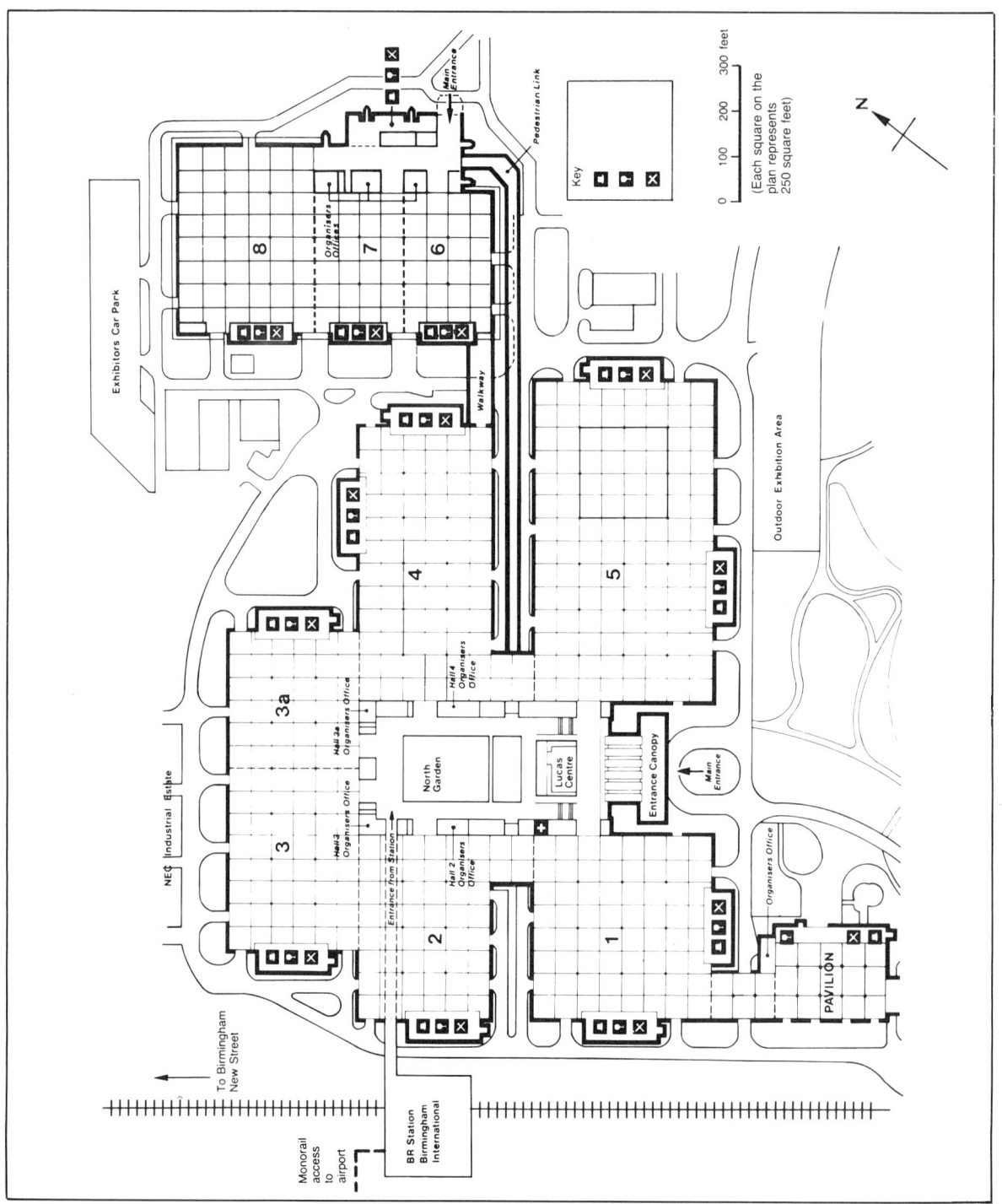

▲ 15.1 *Plan of part of the NEC site*

1 Plan **15.1** is a plan of the NEC Exhibition Halls.

1. Using the scale and your ruler, work out the size of the Pavilion. This is one of the smallest halls. How does it compare in size with a football pitch or a netball court?

2. Most of the halls have symbols to show their facilities. What do you think they mean? On your own copy of plan **15.1** fill in the key.

2 1. Mr Big wishes to set up a computer exhibition. He wants restaurant facilities, easy access to car parking for the exhibitors and 12,000 square feet of space. Use the key and scale to work out which hall he should choose.

2. Some of Mr Big's clients are arriving at the International airport. Write an instruction sheet to direct them to the hall. Use the words right and left in your instructions.

3 What could be exhibited in the Outdoor Exhibition Area?

4 Why does the NEC need an industrial estate? What sort of things could be made there for exhibitions?

> **Now try this . . .**
>
> Hall 5 is the largest hall and has two lots of facilities. Use the scale to work out how big it is. Using graph paper, make a plan of the hall. Mark on it where you would place stands for 20 exhibitors. Leave space for visitors to wander around easily.
>
> Which stands do you think would be in the best position to attract visitors' attention? Explain your choice.

1. BRITISH ISLES

16. DIVERSION AHEAD:
Route planning

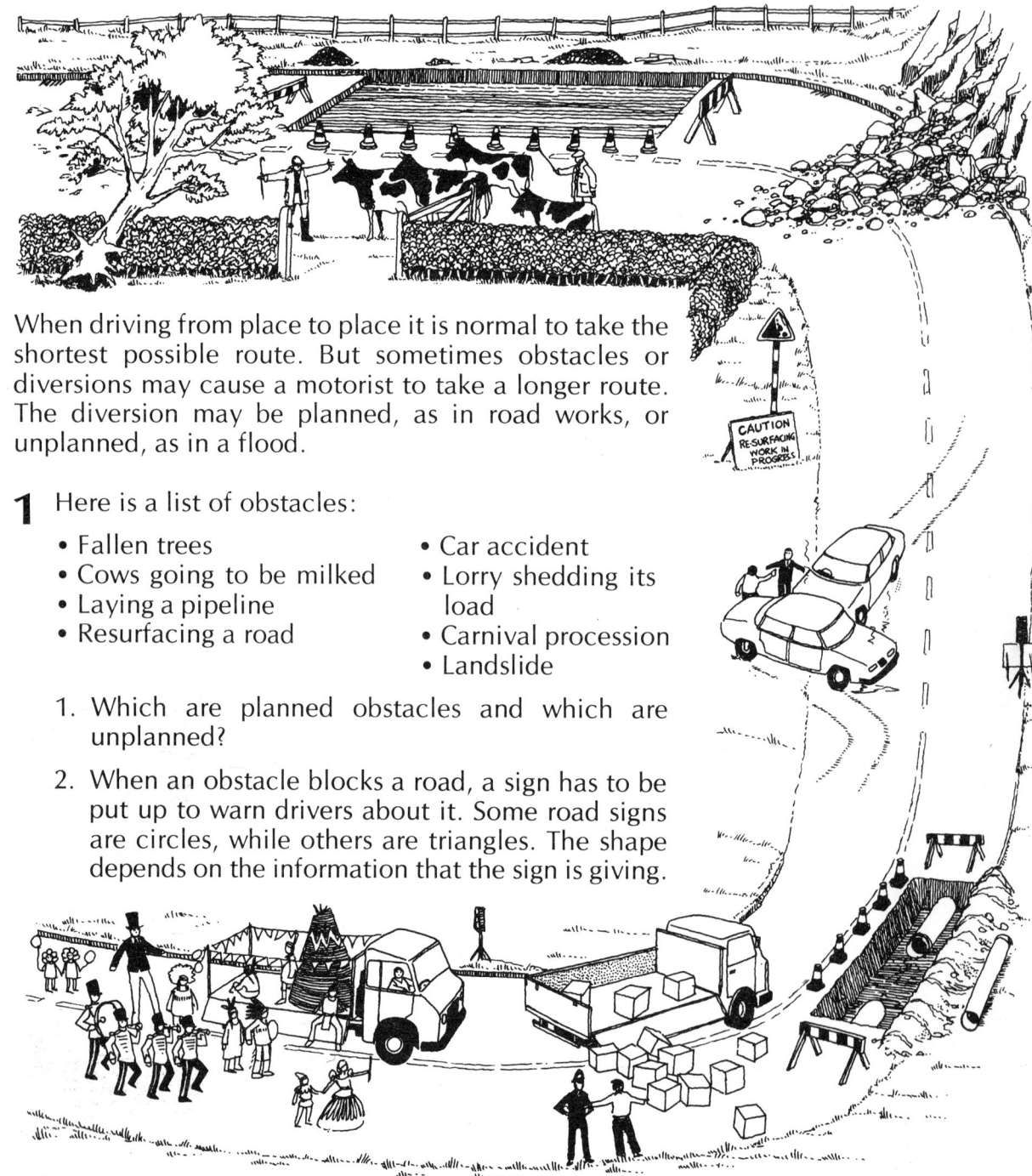

When driving from place to place it is normal to take the shortest possible route. But sometimes obstacles or diversions may cause a motorist to take a longer route. The diversion may be planned, as in road works, or unplanned, as in a flood.

1 Here is a list of obstacles:

- Fallen trees
- Cows going to be milked
- Laying a pipeline
- Resurfacing a road
- Car accident
- Lorry shedding its load
- Carnival procession
- Landslide

1. Which are planned obstacles and which are unplanned?

2. When an obstacle blocks a road, a sign has to be put up to warn drivers about it. Some road signs are circles, while others are triangles. The shape depends on the information that the sign is giving.

Do you know which shape is used for warning signs? (You might find it helpful to look at the Highway Code or at the road signs in Unit 7 of this book.)

3. Make up some road signs to warn motorists about the obstacles in the list. Make sure that you use the correct shape when you draw them.

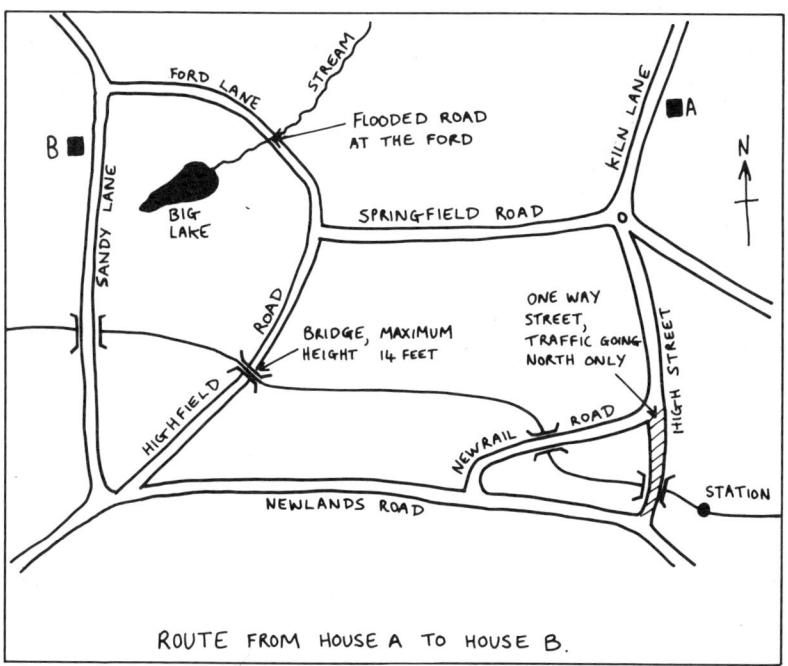

▲ 16.1

2 Look at the sketch-map **16.1**.

Your family is moving from House A in Kiln Lane to House B in Sandy Lane. The removal van is 14 feet 6 inches high, and as you can see on the map there are three main obstacles in the area.

Give instructions to the van driver on how to get from House A to House B, avoiding the obstacles. You could start 'Turn left as you go out of the drive. . . .'

Your turn . . .

Make up a diversion map of your own. Try to put in two planned and two unplanned obstacles. Describe your route between two points.

Further Tasks... on route planning can be found on Worksheet 16.

1. BRITISH ISLES

17. ALL ABOARD THE NARROWBOAT:
Britain's waterways

Canals and **navigable** rivers link up many of the biggest towns and cities in England. Today these canals are largely used by holiday-makers.

Boats can travel at an average speed of three miles per hour around England's canals. Where the level of the land changes, there are **locks**. It takes about ten minutes to pass through a lock. In the busy summer season there may be a queue.

1 A round trip for energetic boaters! Follow the trip in **17.2** on map **17.1**.

▲ *Napton Lock on the Oxford Canal*

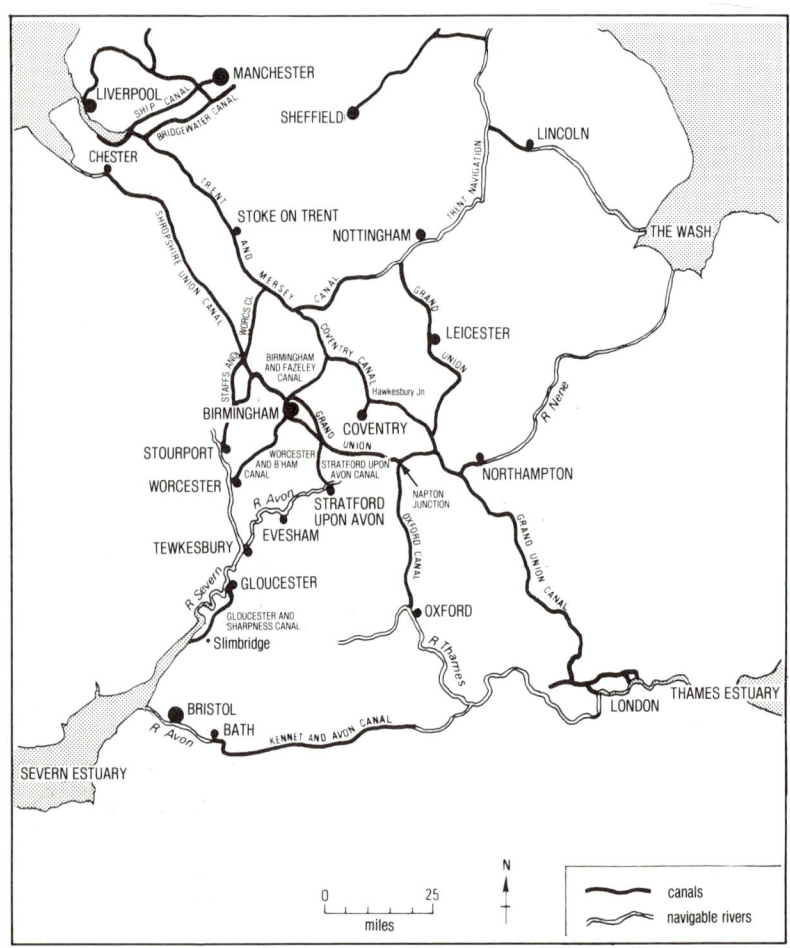

Hire the boat in Oxford. Take the Oxford Canal to Napton Junction, then go east along the Grand Union Canal. Turn north along the Coventry Canal, passing Hawkesbury Junction, and then on to the Birmingham and Fazeley Canal. Take the Grand Union Canal back to Napton Junction. Rejoin the Oxford Canal and finally hand the boat back at Oxford.

▲ 17.2

◀ **17.1** *The canal network in part of England*

The distance you will have covered is 106 miles and you will have gone through 88 locks.

1. How long would you need to hire the boat for if you were travelling for seven hours a day at an average speed of three miles per hour?

2. What other canal or river loops would you like to add to this journey?

3. How many more days would you need to hire the boat for to complete this longer journey?

2 On your own copy of grid **17.3** fill in the answers to the following clues. If your answers are correct the shaded squares will spell a means of transport on canals and rivers. You can find out all the answers from map **17.1**.

1. This river joins the Wash to the Grand Union Canal.
2. This canal goes almost all the way from London to Nottingham.
3. This town is at the southerly end of the Worcester and Birmingham Canal.
4. More than four canal links enter this city.
5. This canal forms a link between the Trent and Mersey Canal and the Grand Union Canal.
6. This canal joins the Trent and Mersey Canal south of Manchester.
7. The Kennet and Avon Canal starts here.
8. This town is at the junction of a river and a canal.
9. This river is navigable (suitable for boats) from Tewkesbury to Stratford.
10. This river flows through Nottingham.

A poster . . .

Read paragraph **17.4**. Make a poster to advise people how to use the canal. It will be displayed in every hired boat.

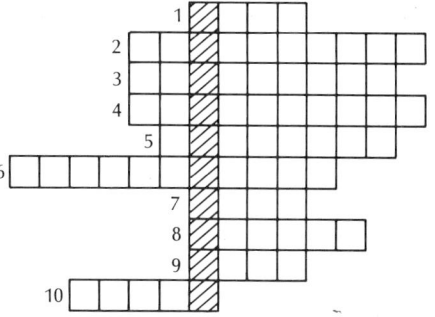

▲ 17.3

A canal holiday is a superb and relaxing way to see the countryside, but some people do not keep to the speed limit. Canals were not built for motorboats, and so the banks are easily worn away. Canal users must be careful not to waste water by leaving lock gates open. In times of drought, movement through locks will usually be restricted. Some canals are getting clogged up with rubbish, so please do not drop anything into the water.

▲ 17.4

1. BRITISH ISLES

18. SEVEN SISTERS:
A country park

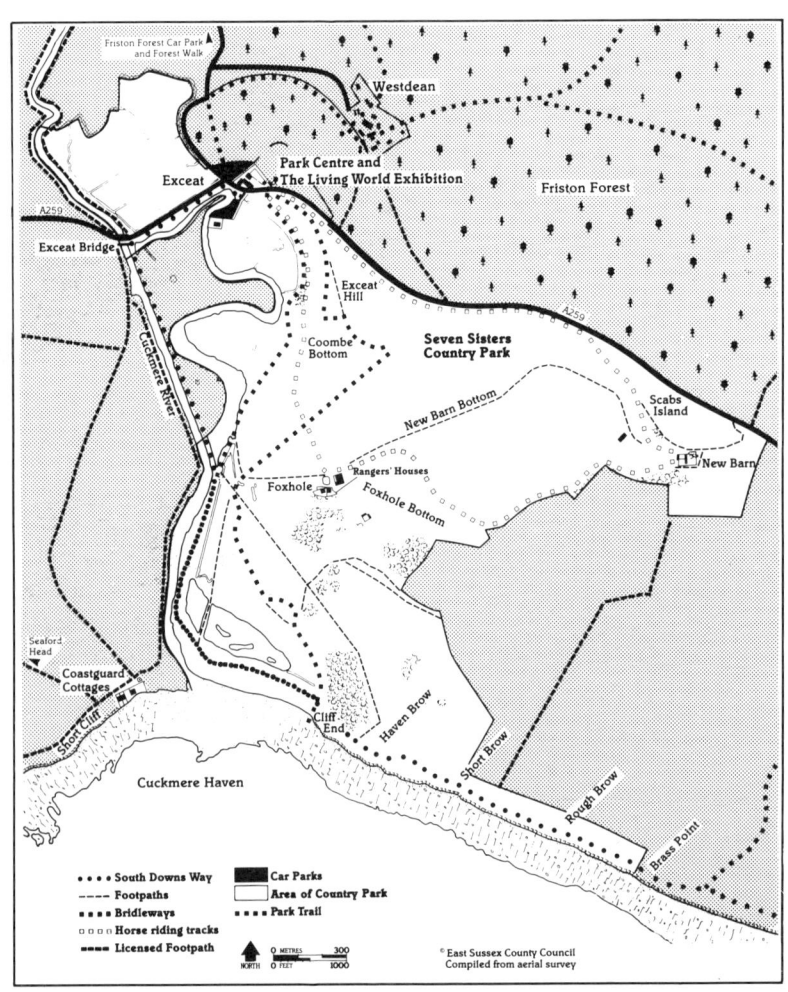

◀ **18.1** *The Seven Sisters Country Park*

Map **18.1** is a map of the Seven Sisters Country Park. It is between Seaford and Eastbourne on the south coast of England. It belongs to the East Sussex County Council. The council aims to conserve the beauty and wildlife of the area while allowing people to enjoy it.

1 Visitors get around the park on foot. Cars are only allowed into the car park areas. Can you suggest why this is? There are several reasons.

2 On map **18.1** you can see footpaths and horse riding tracks. There are also opportunities to study wildlife, for example to watch birds. You can also camp, fish, canoe, row and swim in different areas of the park. On your own copy of the map, label where you think these activities might take place.

Country parks are increasing in number in many regions. They are not always popular with everyone. Why might farmers, local residents and conservationists sometimes object? Worksheet 18 investigates this issue.

Local report . . .

Visit your local park. It may be in the town or the country. List the **amenities** (things provided for the public such as tennis courts, park seats or litter bins).

What age groups does the park cater for best: children, teenagers, the middle-aged or the old? Write a short report on how you would improve the park.

1. BRITISH ISLES

19. SANDCASTLES AND SUN LOUNGERS:
Planning holiday activities

Torquay is a tourist resort on the south coast of Devon. Together with the surrounding towns it is known as the English Riviera.

There is plenty to do in Torquay. The harbour area is a very busy part of the town. If you look at the town plan **19.1**, you can see the moorings of the marina inside the harbour wall.

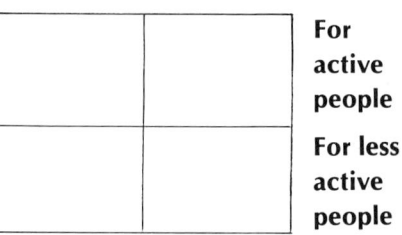

▲ 19.2

1
1. Find the harbour area on the town plan **19.1**. Make a list of all the activities you can do in that half mile square round the harbour. Then copy grid **19.2**. Place each activity in the correct box.

2. Why would Meadfoot beach be a good place for drivers who can't walk far? Why is Redgate beach less easy to get to?

2
1. Babbacombe Road stretches from the museum in Torquay to the two car parks near the model village. Measure how long it is using a piece of string and the scale.

2. Using the directions 'right', 'left' and 'straight on', describe how to get from the information centre by the Pavilion to the squash courts in Old Woods Hill, which is in the north-west corner of the map.

3. If you were looking for a quiet place to stay, which area would you choose? Why?

4. If you wanted to windsurf all the time, in which area would you stay?

Many people in towns such as Torquay have worked hard to develop and improve tourist facilities. They want to attract more people to their area. Some towns manage to attract many more tourists than others. Can you think of any features that make a town such as Torquay attractive to tourists? Worksheet 19 explores this issue.

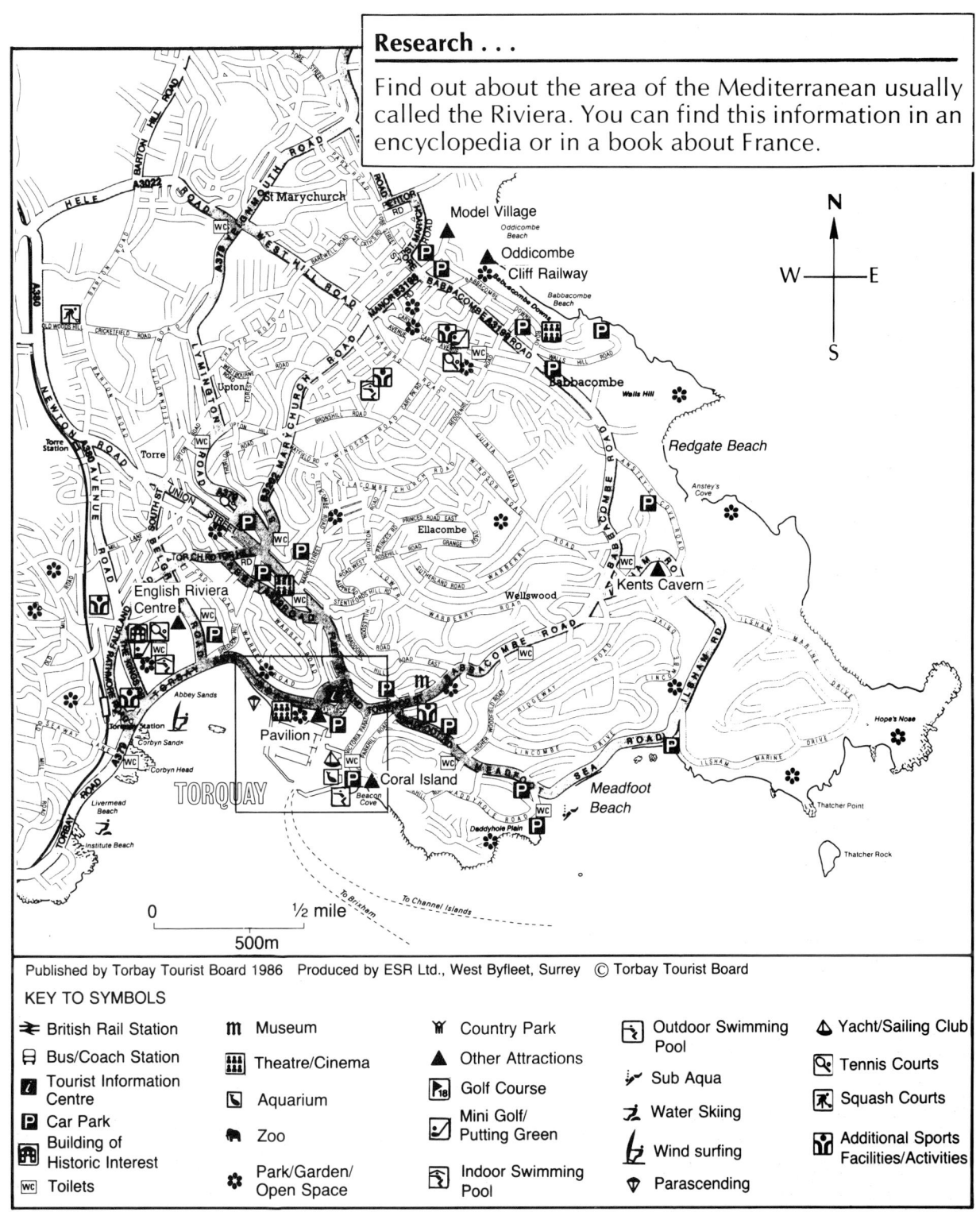

▲ 19.1 *Town plan of Torquay*

1. BRITISH ISLES

20. HOW FAR?
National Parks in England and Wales

Many people take their holidays in National Parks: climbing the peaks, boating on the lakes, horse-riding on the moors, bird-watching on the coastal cliffs or just sightseeing.

The first National Park in Britain – the Peak District – was set up in 1949. The aim was to let people use the area but at the same time to **preserve** the beauty of the countryside and to **conserve** the land for the future. The land in the parks is owned by farmers, the Forestry Commission, the Water Companies and many private landowners.

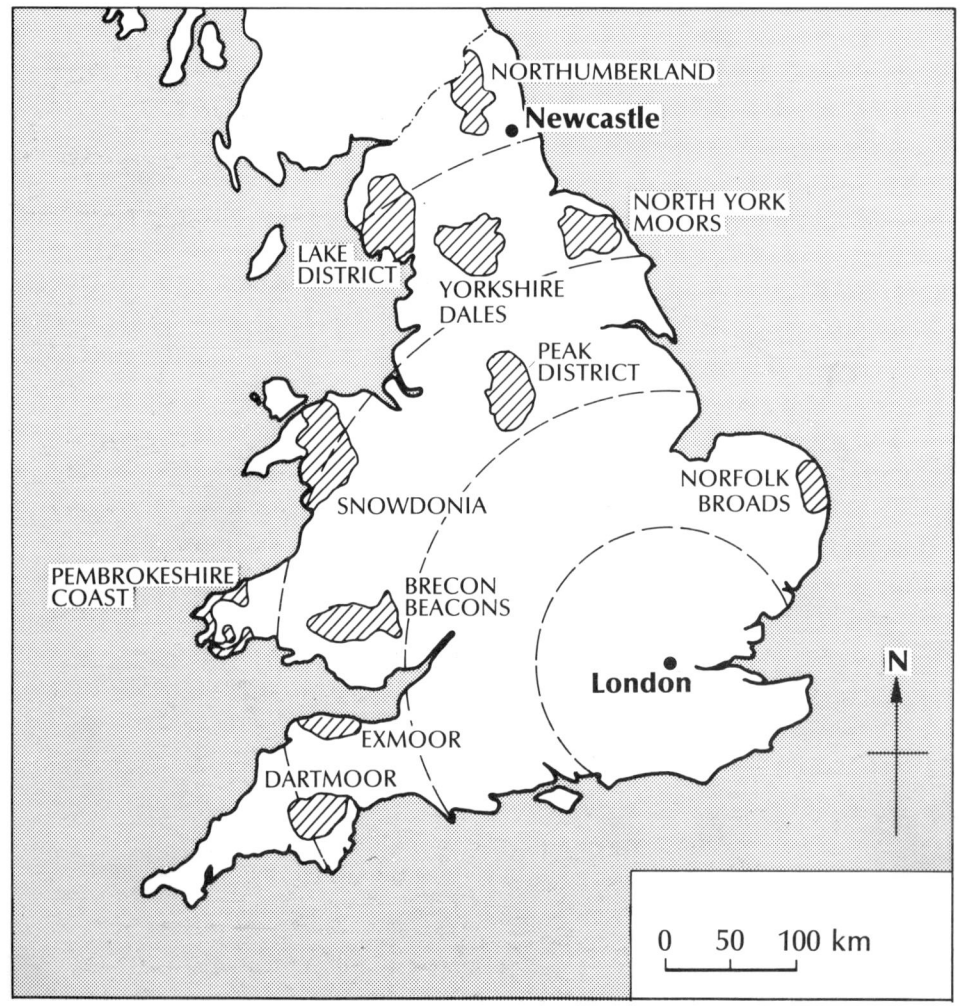

◀ 20.1 *National Parks in England and Wales*

44

1 On map **20.1** you can see **isolines** (lines showing equal distance from a place). In this case the lines are drawn every 100 kilometres from the centre of London. For example, all the points on the third line are 300 km from London.

1. Which National Park is furthest from London?
2. How far is the Peak District from London?

2 Most of the Parks are too far from London to make a day trip worthwhile. It would be time to come home as soon as you arrived. But if you live in Newcastle, for example, you are more fortunate.

1. Trace map **20.1** and, using a compass and the scale at the bottom of the map, draw 100 kilometre isolines (circles) from Newcastle.
2. How far from Newcastle is Dartmoor?
3. Which parks can you reach most easily?

3 Diagram **20.2** shows some of the activities that go on in the Snowdonia National Park in Wales, scrambled up. Unfortunately, many of these activities clash with other interests in the Park, such as conservation.

1. Unscramble the words. Then choose the activity you think is most important. Work out why you think it should be allowed to continue in the Park.
2. Other people in the class may choose different activities. Hold a debate to compare the reasons for your choices.

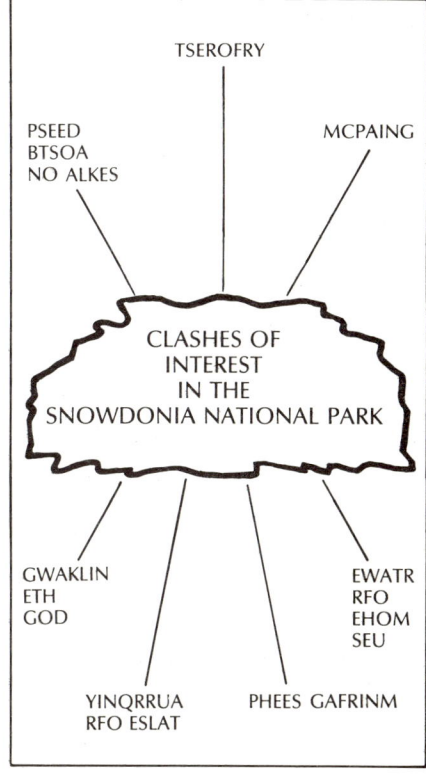

▲ 20.2

Find out ...

With a partner, use an atlas to find out:

1. In which county is the Pembrokeshire National Park?
2. Which two National Parks include part of the Pennines?
3. Which counties have two National Parks within them?

Further Tasks... on the Norfolk Broads National Park and Scotland's National Scenic Areas are on Worksheets 20A and 20B.

1. BRITISH ISLES

21. DOWN THE TUBE:
Tyne and Wear Metro & the London Underground

There are two underground railway systems in England: the London Underground and the Tyne and Wear Metro in Newcastle. Both systems connect with the British Rail overground network.

Travellers find their way by looking at a route diagram which is a **topological map**. The shapes on these maps are simplified. Map **21.1** shows the true shape of the River Tyne. Map **21.2** is the topological map of the Tyne and Wear Metro, including the river.

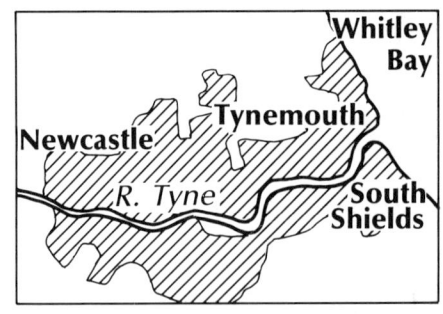

▲ 21.1 The Tyne and Wear Metro

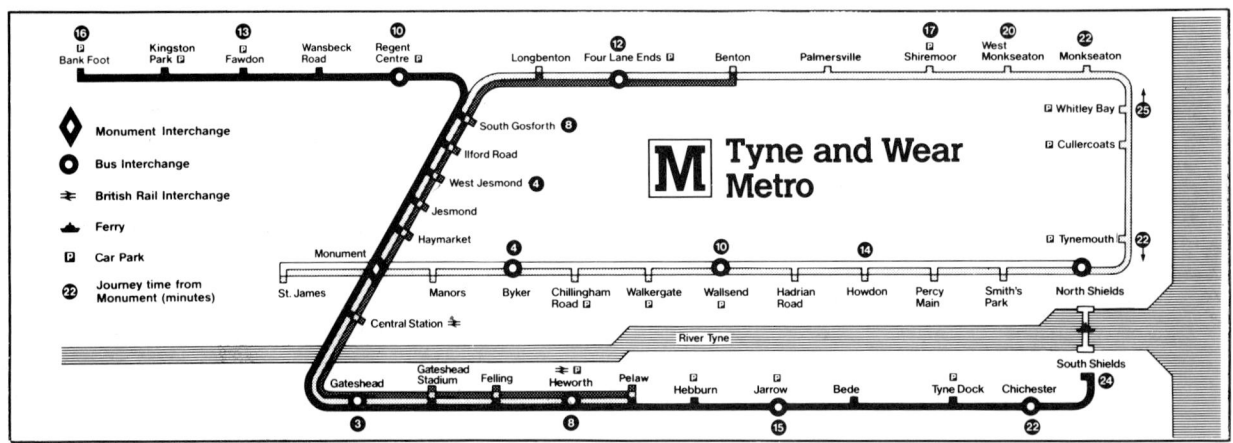

▲ 21.2 The Tyne and Wear Metro

1 Look at map **21.2**, the map of the Tyne and Wear Metro. A family from Durham, the Wards, are travelling to Whitley Bay for a day by the sea. They catch a British Rail train and arrive at the Central Station, where they change to the Metro.

1. How many Metro stations do they pass through between Central Station and Whitley Bay?

2. Copy out table **21.3** and fill in the station names on the right in the correct columns:

Central Station
Tynemouth
Chichester
Heworth
Kingston Park
Byker

British Rail interchange	Car parking	Bus interchange

▲ 21.3

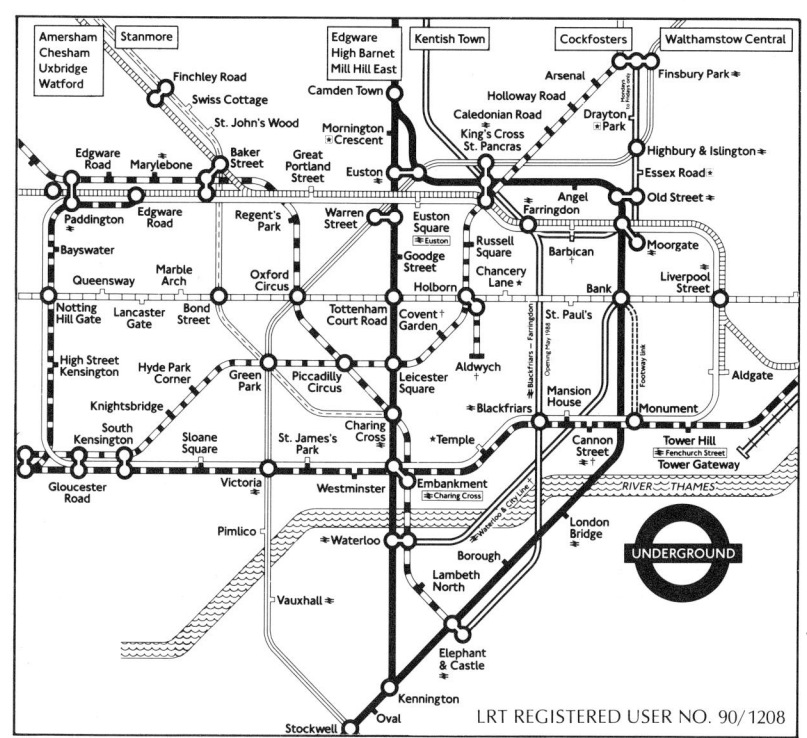
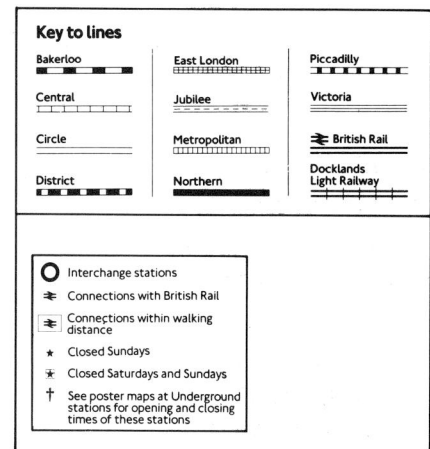

▲ 21.4 *Part of the London Underground*

2 Map **21.4** is the central area of the London Underground.

1. A group of students from Birmingham arrive at Euston station to visit London. Their plans for the day are shown in **21.5**. They have also made notes on how to get from place to place on the Underground. Is their route correct? Check each stage on map **21.4**.

2. Using map **21.4**, work out a route for a day trip starting and finishing at Waterloo. Visit the London Dungeon (London Bridge station), The Guinness World of Records (Piccadilly Circus) and the Museum of the Moving Image (Waterloo).

Try this . . .

Use the two Underground maps, **21.2** and **21.4**, to make up a quiz. Work out a route like the one in **21.5**, but leave some stations or lines blank. Ask someone else to work out what the missing stages are.

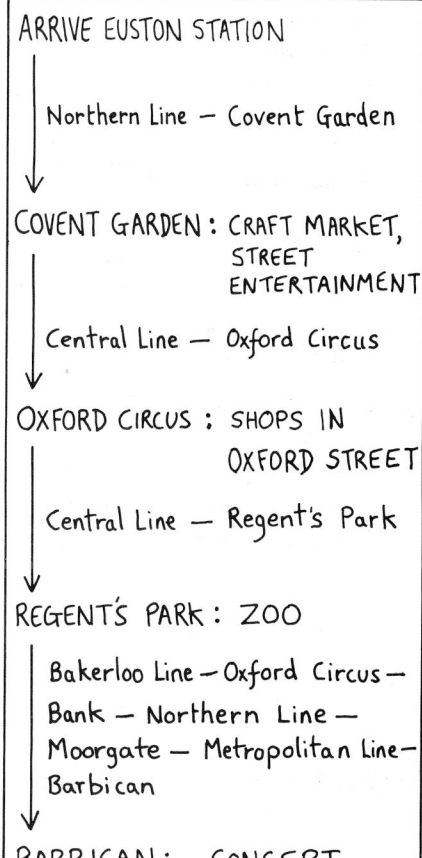

▲ 21.5

47

1. BRITISH ISLES

22. ALL ABOARD FOR FRENCH BREAD:
Channel crossings

1 Map **22.1** shows the position of ports on both sides of the English Channel. Copy out tables **22.2** and **22.3** and, using an atlas, match the correct letters and numbers to the names of the ports. Mark them on your own copy of map **22.1**.

English ports	
Portsmouth	
Dover	
Folkestone	
Ramsgate	
Newhaven	
Southampton	
Sheerness	

▲ **22.2**

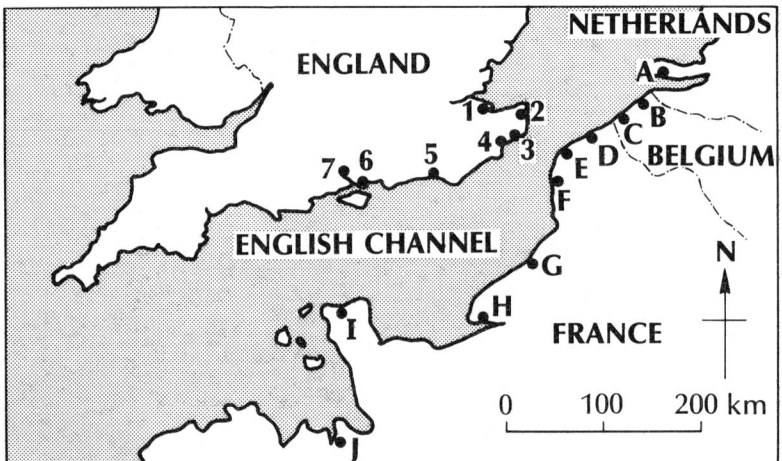

▲ 22.1 *Channel ports*

Continental ports	
St Malo	
Calais	
Cherbourg	
Boulogne	
Dieppe	
Ostend	
Zeebrugge	
Le Havre	
Dunkerque	
Flushing	

▲ **22.3**

2 The pie chart, **22.4**, shows Channel crossings from the busiest of the English Channel ports for a weekday in July. Using the pie chart, answer the following questions:

  1. Which of the English ports has the greatest number of crossings in one day?
  2. Which two of these English ports have the greatest choice of cross-channel destinations?

3 Now, using tables **22.5** and **22.6** and an atlas, answer these questions:

  1. If you are travelling to Paris, which of the two French ports in table **22.6** is closest to the capital?
  2. What is the fastest way of going by sea from England to France? How long does it take?
  3. Which port do you leave from and which do you arrive at?

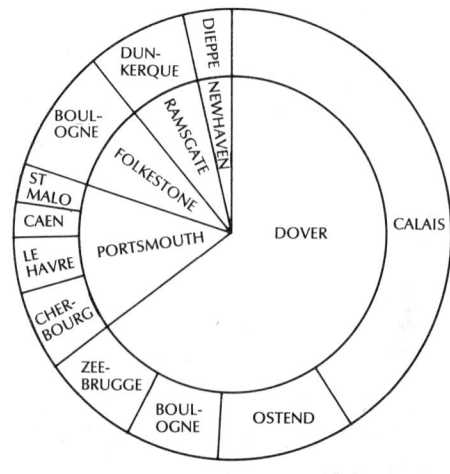

▲ **22.4**

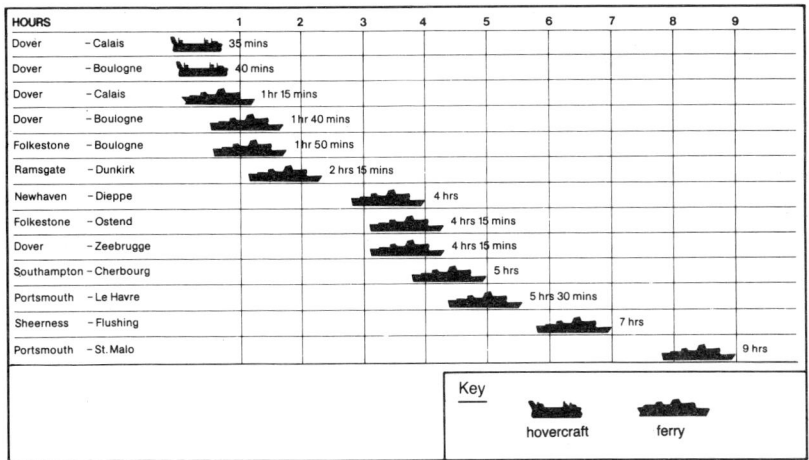

▲ 22.5 *Duration of Channel crossings*

4. Table **22.5** shows a different way of travelling between the same two ports. How much slower is this?

5. If you wanted to drive to Marbella on the Spanish coast which would be the shortest car journey: Calais to Marbella or Boulogne to Marbella?

6. What would be the advantage of taking the ferry from Portsmouth to St Malo?

Next...

Some of the ports mentioned in this unit – e.g. Southampton and Portsmouth – are used by cargo ships as well as passenger ferries. Most ports specialise in either cargo or passenger ships.

Use an atlas and an encyclopedia to find out:
a) where the following ports are located

   Felixstowe   Hull   Harwich   Liverpool

b) whether they specialise in passenger or cargo ships.

MILEAGE GUIDE

	CALAIS	BOULOGNE
Amsterdam	223	249
Barcelona	865	835
Basle	483	476
Berlin	574	598
Bordeaux	550	506
Brussels	122	146
Cannes	743	712
Cologne	253	269
Copenhagen	661	686
Esbjerg	640	664
Faro	1,393	1,362
Florence	887	850
Frankfurt	371	387
Geneva	506	475
Hamburg	475	510
Hanover	408	427
Innsbruck	684	663
Lisbon	1,318	1,287
Luxembourg	256	260
Lyons	469	438
Madrid	994	963
Marbella	1,375	1,344
Marseilles	664	633
Milan	694	673
Munich	614	593
Nice	761	730
Paris	182	151
Rome	1,059	1,029
Salzburg	700	679
Strasbourg	393	386
Venice	863	837
Vienna	820	835

▲ 22.6 *Distances from Calais and Boulogne*

Travelling to the Continent may well be much quicker once the Channel Tunnel is open. But not everyone thinks the Channel Tunnel is a good idea, and its developers have had many problems. Are there any problems that you have heard about? Worksheet 22 explores this issue.

2. EUROPE

23. TO THE LAND OF THE VIKINGS:
Scandinavia

Norway, with Sweden and Denmark, makes up the area called Scandinavia. Norway is famous for its coastline of **fjords** and islands. The fjords are drowned valleys carved out by **glaciers**.

A holiday in Norway is an adventure. Travelling around might include journeys by coastal steamer, ferry boat, air and rail as well as by road.

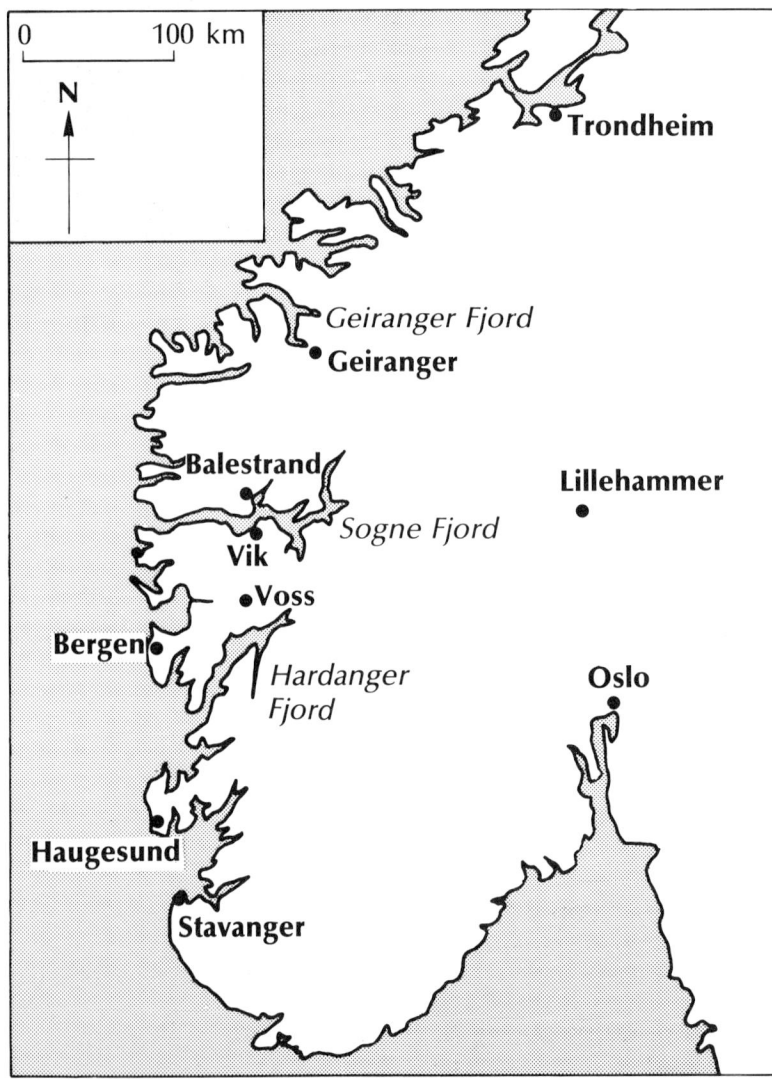

▲ 23.1 Southern Norway

▲ Hardanger Fjord, Norway

1 Map **23.1** shows southern Norway. On your own copy, mark the routes taken on the following holiday trips. Use a different colour for each route.
Trip A: Bergen to Haugesund, then to Stavanger, by boat.
Trip B: From Bergen to Voss by train. Then by coach to Vik, and back to Bergen by boat.
Trip C: From Oslo to Lillehammer by coach, then by coach to Geiranger. To Balestrand by boat then on to Bergen.

2 Which Scandinavian country are these facts about? Take the first letter of the fourth word in each sentence to make up the answer.

1. The farms produce dairy products such as cream, cheese and butter, as well as bacon.
2. The port of Esbjerg is on the west coast.
3. Legoland provides a nice day out for the family.
4. The famous Little Mermaid statue sits on a rock in Copenhagen harbour.
5. One tourist city, Aarhus, is on the mainland, Jutland.
6. Copenhagen is the reason for many people's visit.
7. Its currency is krone.

▲ *The Little Mermaid*

How would you travel? . . .

Collect several travel brochures about Sweden. Find out as many ways as possible to get there. For example, one way of travelling to Gothenburg in Sweden is by boat. From Newcastle, the journey takes 26 hours.

1. Which would be the most convenient route from your home?
2. Would your decision depend on whether you were going to the capital, Stockholm, or somewhere else?
3. Would there be much difference in price between the different routes?

2. EUROPE

24. THE FRENCH CONNECTION:
French railways

1 A group of students are travelling from London to Bordeaux. They decide to leave London Victoria station on 26 October. They plan to cross the Channel around midday. Their train timetable, **24.1**, is complicated. They need help in working out the answers to the following questions:

1. What is the departure time from Dover?
2. Will they travel by ship or hovercraft? (Refer to the key.)
3. What time do they leave Boulogne?
4. Which Paris station will they arrive at?

LONDON → Amiens/Rouen-PARIS

Dates of Operation	Daily 23 Oct-2 Nov 23 Dec-8 Jan not 26 Dec	Daily 25 Sep-22 Oct	Mon to Fri from 24 Oct not 31 Oct 1 and 11 Nov 26 Dec	Mon to Fri 26 Sep 21 Oct	Daily 23 Oct-24 Dec 2-29 Jan and 13 Feb-25 Mar	Daily 25 Sep-2 Oct and 16-22 Oct	Daily 26 Mar	Daily from 23 Oct not 26 Dec	Daily 25 Sep-22 Oct	Daily from 23 Oct not 26 Dec	Daily 25 Sep-22 Oct	Daily from 17 Mar	Daily 23 Oct 16 Mar not 26 Dec	Daily 25 Sep-22 Oct	Daily from 23 Oct	Daily 25 Sep-22 Oct	Daily from 17 Mar	Daily 23 Oct-24 Dec 2-29 Jan and from 13 Feb	Daily 25 Sep-2 Oct and 16-22 Oct	Daily 3-15 Oct 27-30 Dec 1 Jan and 30 Jan-12 Feb
London Victoria d	0745	0830	0900	1000	0825	0902	0804	1000	1100	1120	1220	1200	1300	1400	1410	1510	1410	2040	2140	2300
Folkestone Harbour d	🛥	🛥	🛥	🛥	🛥	🛥	🛥	🛥	🛥	🛥	🛥	🛥	🛥	🛥	🛥	🛥	🛥	🛥	🛥	🛥
Dover Hoverport d	1000	1100	—	—	—	—	—	1205	1305	—	—	1330	1430	—	1405	1505	1605	—	1705	—	—	—
Dover Western Docks d	—	—	1130	1230	—	—	—	—	—	—	—	—	—	—	—	—	—	1630	1730	—	—	—	0215
Newhaven d	—	—	—	—	1015	1100	1000	—	—	—	—	—	—	—	—	—	—	—	2230	2330	—
Train no.	2020		2026		308			2022		404		2028	2036		400		2046	200		2006
Calais Maritime d	—		1426		—	—	—	—	—	—	—	—	—	—	1932	—	—	—	—	0525
Boulogne Hoverport d	1200		—		—	—	—	1410	—	—	—	1609	1715	—	—	1913	—	—	—
Boulogne Maritime d	—		—		—	—	—	—	—	1645	—	—	—	—	—	—	—	—	—
Dieppe Maritime d	—		—		1554	—	—	—	—	—	—	—	—	—	—	—	0438	—	—
Rouen a	—		—		—	1647	—	—	—	—	—	—	—	—	—	—	0530	—
Amiens a	1311		1611		—	—	—	1521	—	1807	—	1716	1827	—	2112	—	2020	—	—	0728
Paris St Lazare a	—		—		1816	—	—	—	—	—	—	—	—	—	—	—	—	0703	—
Nord a	1418		1724		—	—	—	1632	—	1920	—	1826	1929	—	2228	—	2124	—	—	0844

▲ 24.1

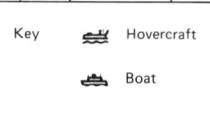

Key 🛫 Hovercraft
     🛥 Boat

Connections from PARIS

Train no.		313	4633	123	5051	737	471	4071	4051	77	EC 27 ℝ	747 ℝ	5061	647 ℝ	4415	307	175
Paris Lyon	d	–	–	–	0937	1000	–	–	–	–	1806	1828	2045	2100	–	–	–
Austerlitz	d	0842	0903	0930	–		1003	1730	1730	1800					2106	2230	2253
Tours	a		1148		–			1930									
Dijon	a		–		1203			–			1944		2348				
Lyon Part-Dieu	a		–		–	1202		–			–	2032	–	2304			
Grenoble	a		–		–	1317		–			–	2146	–				
Bordeaux	a	1309	–		–	–		–	2242		–	–	–	–			
Toulouse	a	–	–		–	–	1650	–	–	2359	–	–	–	–	0428		0700
Lourdes	a	–	–	1636	–	–	–	–	–	–	–	–	–	–	–	0715	–

▲ 24.2

2 For the next part of their journey they need to consult timetable **24.2**. Like London, Paris has many different stations, serving different parts of France. The students need to cross Paris to get to the station that serves the Bordeaux region.

1. Which Paris station does the Bordeaux train number 4051 depart from?
2. How much time do they have to cross Paris to catch this train?
3. What time do they arrive in Bordeaux?
4. How long does it take to travel from London to Bordeaux?
5. Could they travel on the same train to Toulouse and Lourdes?
6. Which train would they have to catch from Paris if they wanted to go to Lourdes instead of Bordeaux?
7. How long does the journey to Lourdes take?

Continuez ...

Map **24.3** is a **topological** map of railways in France. It shows the connections between towns, but the towns are not in their true positions. Use an atlas to find out the correct position of each town shown in the topological map. Mark it on your own outline map of France.

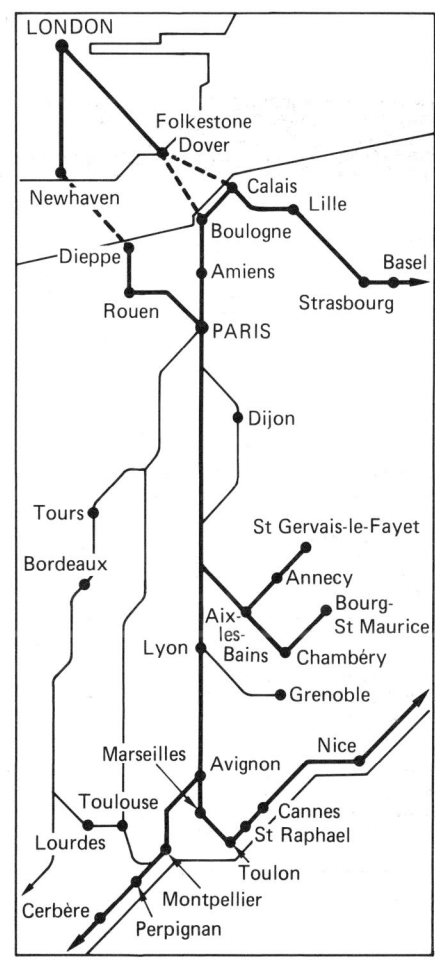

▲ 24.3 French railways

2. EUROPE

25. ESCAPE TO THE SUN:
Holidays in France

August is holiday month in Paris. Many Parisians go away for the first two weeks in August. Some go for the whole month. They head for the country or the coast. In which direction do you think most people travel? Why?

With most people going away at the same time, serious traffic jams can build up on **autoroutes** (motorways) such as the Autoroute du Soleil.

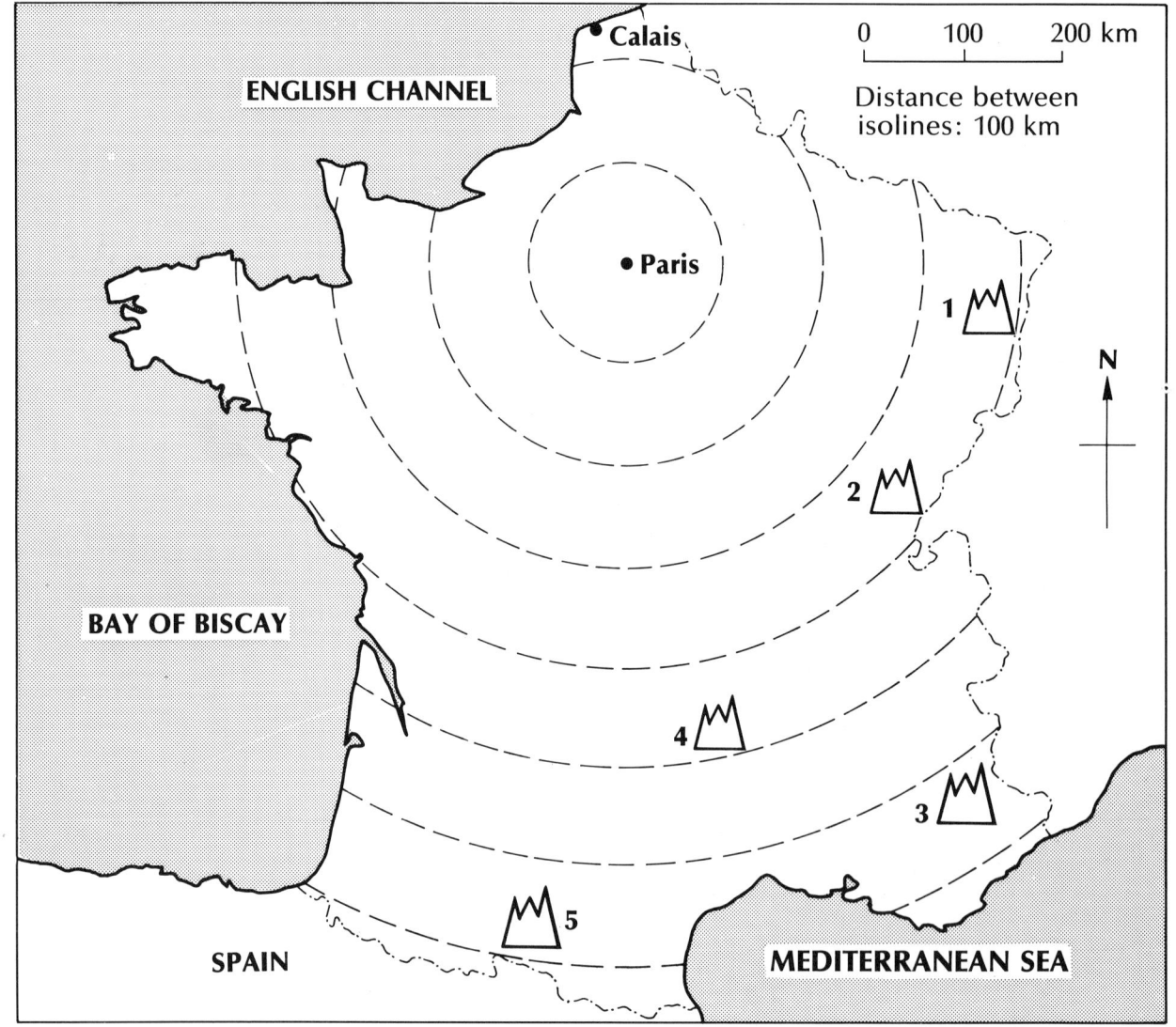

▲ 25.1 *Distances from Paris to other parts of France*

1 Isoline map **25.1** shows the distance from Paris to other parts of France.

1. How far is it from Paris to the Mediterranean coast?
2. Which seaside areas are nearest to Paris?
3. How far away are they?

2 The isolines on map **25.1** are drawn at the same intervals as those on map **20.1** of the National Parks in England and Wales, in Unit 20. This makes it easy to compare the distances from London to other parts of Britain with those from Paris to other parts of France. How much further could you travel in France, from Paris, than in England and Wales, from London, without crossing the sea?

3 Instead of going to the coast for a holiday, you might prefer the mountains. Five mountain areas of France are marked on map **25.1**. Use an atlas to help you unscramble the names on the right and match them to the numbers on map **25.1**.

PALS
FSSMIA TRLCAEN
RAJU
SGVSOE
SYREEEPN

More . . .

1. The fact that most Parisians take their holidays in August, and travel on the first Saturday in the month, causes problems other than traffic jams. What effect do you think it will have on:
   • motorway service stations
   • towns 'en route' to the tourist areas
   • Paris during August
   • airports and railway stations?

2. What advantages are there in a slightly more staggered holiday season, as in Britain?

3. What problems does a seaside resort in a holiday area face if most holiday-makers want to visit it during a short season?

2. EUROPE

26. UPSTREAM, DOWNSTREAM:
The Rhine waterway

The River Rhine is a large international waterway. It passes through four countries. The river's **source** is in the Swiss Alps. The Rhine flows to its **mouth**, a **delta**, at Rotterdam, then into the North Sea.

1 Using map **26.1**, and starting at the source in Switzerland, make a list of the countries which the river passes through, or which it borders.

Tourist brochures describe the Rhine as one of the most beautiful rivers in the world. River cruisers take holiday-makers past picturesque castles and vine-clad slopes.

But there are also many industrial towns on the river. It is a very important line of communication through Europe. Large numbers of commercial barges ferry raw materials upstream and manufactured goods downstream.

▲ **26.1** *The River Rhine*

▲ *Castles and cargo in the Rhineland*

2 Use these clues to work out what might be in the barges. Fill in the answers on your own copies of grids **26.2** and **26.3**.

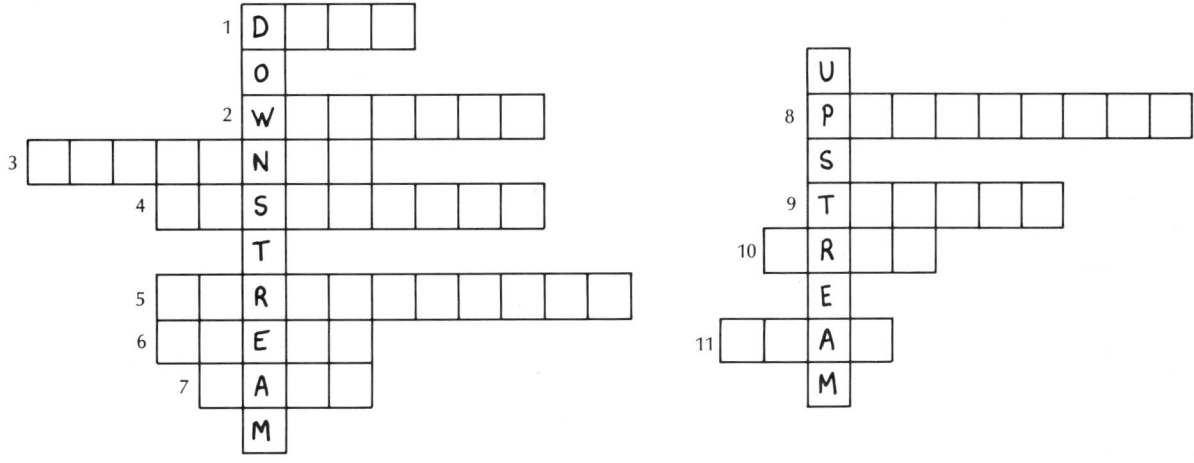

▲ 26.2   ▲ 26.3

1. Chemicals used to colour materials.
2. and 3. Electrical appliances used on dirty clothes.
4. Used for recording music.
5. Chemicals put on fields to make crops grow.
6. You put food in one of these to cook it.
7. Two kinds are Mercedes and Volkswagen.
8. Fuel for motor vehicles – can be refined or crude.
9. Used for making houses, furniture or paper.
10. A raw material for steel.
11. Fuel which is burned in the iron and steel industry and to make electricity.

At the mouth . . .

The place where a river enters the sea is called its **mouth**. The mouth of the River Rhine is a **delta**. The mouths of some other rivers, like the River Thames, are **estuaries**. Find out how a delta is different from an estuary.

57

2. EUROPE

27. WHERE SHALL WE GO?
The Mediterranean

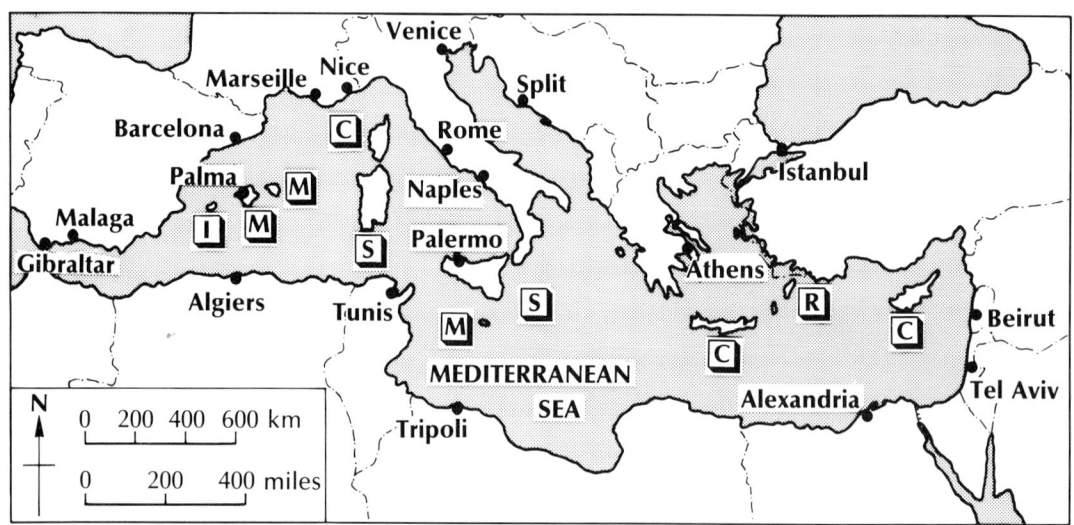

▲ 27.1 The Mediterranean area

1 On your own copy of map **27.1**, name the islands marked with their initial letters and all the countries around the coast of the Mediterranean Sea. Use an atlas. Take care with the islands. Many of them start with the same letter of the alphabet.

2 You can fly between most of the major cities marked on the map. Using the scales on your own copy of the map, copy and complete table **27.2**. Note that some distances are in miles, others are in kilometres.

◀ 27.2

From	To	Distance
Athens	Alexandria	kilometres
Tel Aviv	Athens	miles
Marseille	Palma	kilometres
Malaga	Venice	miles
Istanbul	Beirut	miles
Marseille		1200 kilometres
Barcelona		550 miles
Palermo		450 kilometres

3 If you were flying you would travel in a fairly straight line. If you were cruising or sailing you would sometimes want to go ashore to visit places or pick up supplies.

58

1. Work out the distances between stops on a round trip cruise from Barcelona to Palma, Rome, Palermo and back to Barcelona.

2. Sort out these scrambled place names:
SUITN   NSAETH   MALPA   TSPIL
CNIE   TAMAL
Next, plan a cruise to visit them in a sensible order.

3. Use the scale to work out the total distance for the cruise in kilometres.

4 Which places named on map **27.1** fit these descriptions? You will need to use an atlas.

1. The main city on the island of Majorca in the Balearic Islands.

2. A major port on the south coast of France.

3. The capital city of Italy.

4. A city on the Sea of Marmara.

5. A port in Israel.

6. A city on the north coast of the Adriatic Sea.

Find out . . .

There are fewer resorts on the south side of the Mediterranean Sea than on the north side. Find out about this southern area.

1. Why is it less **developed**?

2. Could it become a major tourist area in the future?

3. If so, what developments would have to take place?

4. Do you think those developments would be a good thing for the area?

The popularity of the Mediterranean has led to a big increase in pollution of the sea and the beaches – enough to worry the governments of the Mediterranean countries. What causes of pollution do you know about? Worksheet 27 looks at how people try to tackle this problem.

2. EUROPE

28. NOW FOR THE SUN:
The Spanish climate

Graph **28.1** shows rainfall and temperature for Barcelona and Birmingham. They are drawn on the same graph so that they can be compared more easily. The temperature is shown by a line graph and rainfall by a bar graph. Map **28.2** shows where Barcelona and Birmingham are.

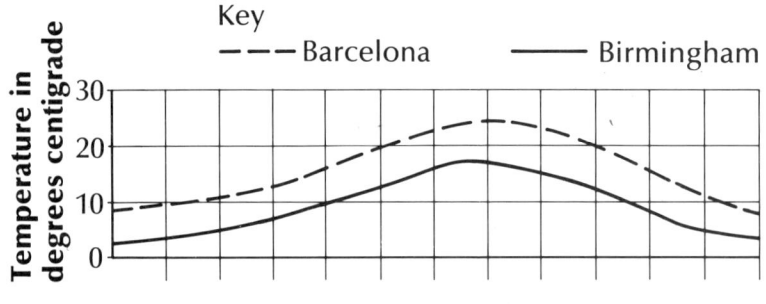

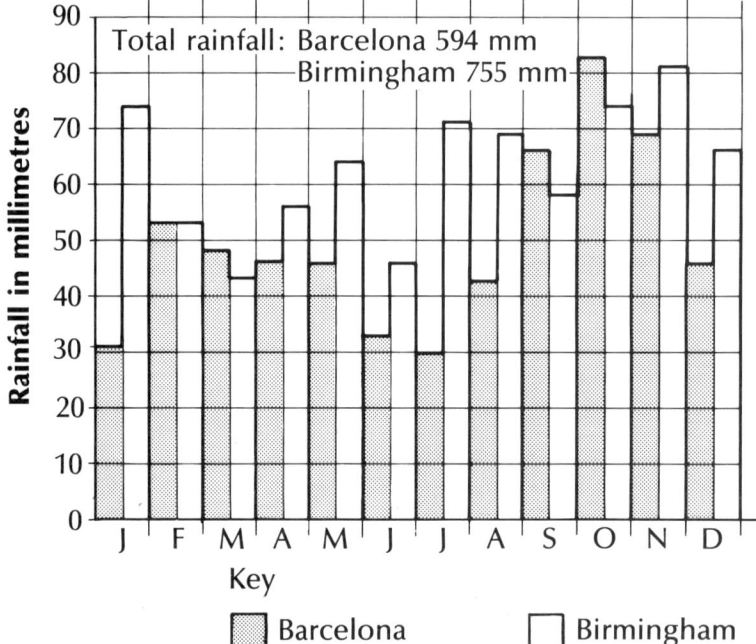

◀ **28.1** Average temperature and total monthly rainfall in Barcelona and Birmingham

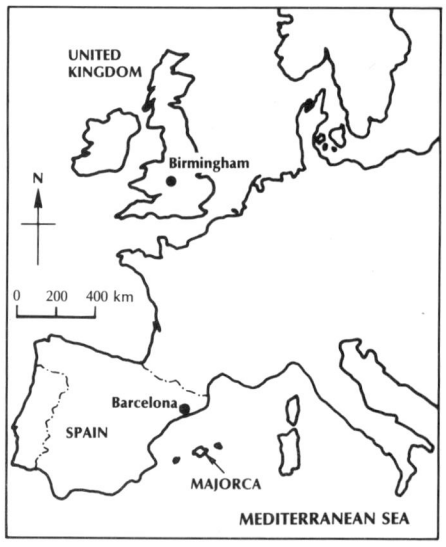

▲ **28.2** Location of Birmingham, Barcelona and Majorca

1 The most popular holiday months in Europe are July and August. The average temperature in Birmingham is about 16 degrees centigrade in July.

　1. What is the average temperature in Barcelona during July?

60

2. Is this the hottest month in Barcelona?

3. In July Birmingham has 70 millimetres of rain on average. What is the rainfall in Barcelona in July?

The answers to these questions will give you a clue as to why Spain is a popular place for British people to go on holiday.

4. Although July and August are the most popular times for holidays, Spain's holiday season continues all the year round. Many retired people go there in December, January and February. Look at the graph and work out why these months are attractive to British visitors.

5. There are three months when Barcelona is wetter than Birmingham. Which months are they?

2 Table **28.3** shows rainfall and temperature figures for Majorca. This is an island in the Mediterranean Sea. It is marked on map **28.2**.

	J	F	M	A	M	J	J	A	S	O	N	D
°C	10	11	12	15	17	21	24	25	23	18	14	11
mm	39	34	51	32	29	17	3	25	55	77	47	40

▲ 28.3

1. On graph paper, draw your own climate graph to represent these figures.

2. Compare this graph with the graph for Barcelona. Which place has the best climate for a holiday resort? Explain the reasons for your answer.

Now collect...

Some newspapers report temperature, rainfall and hours of sunshine every day from cities and resorts all over the world. Collect a variety of newspaper weather reports for one day. Combine them to make a global (world) weather report.

You could imagine what this report would sound like if it was given on the radio's World Service. Record your report on a cassette. You can then repeat the exercise at other times of year and compare the results.

2. EUROPE

29. SUNNY CITIES?
Weather in Europe

Maps **29.1** and **29.2** show the weather forecast for Europe for a day in September. Map **29.1** shows **fronts**. A front happens when a mass of warm air and a mass of cold air meet. A front can bring cold or warm weather. When a front passes overhead, it usually brings rain.

◀ 29.1 Weather forecast, 26 September

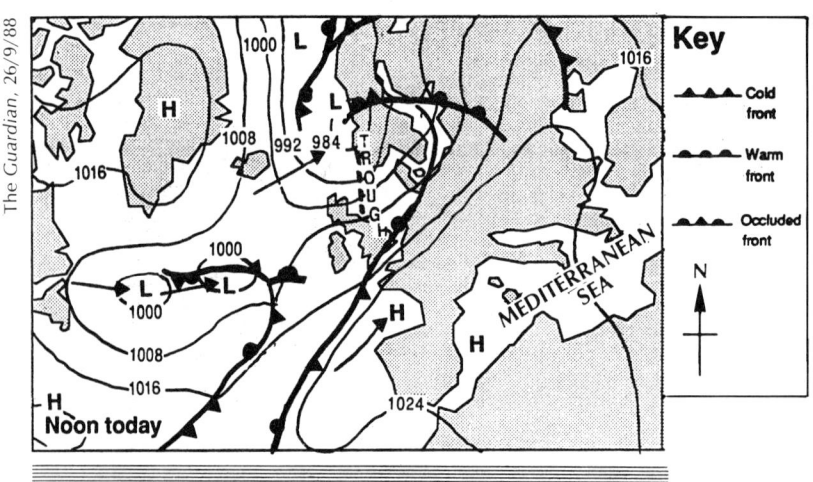

Beyond Britain

◀ 29.2 Weather forecast, 26 September

Map **29.1** also shows **isobars**, which are lines showing equal pressure. Winds are strongest when the isobars are closest together.

1 Look carefully at the two maps. Map **29.1** shows a larger area than map **29.2**.

1. What kind of front is causing rainfall over Copenhagen?
2. Do you think it is wet or dry in London?

The area round the Mediterranean Sea is having good weather. The pressure is high (**H**) at 1024 millibars. Map **29.2** shows that the temperature in Rome is 27 degrees centigrade (°C).

3. On the west coast of Norway the letter **L** and the word **trough** show that the pressure is low. What is the pressure in millibars?
4. What effect is this area of low pressure having on weather in Oslo and Stockholm?

2 Map **29.3** shows Europe more than a month later.

1. Do you think the weather is wet or dry in London?
2. Look at the weather conditions over the Mediterranean. How are they similar to those on 26 September?

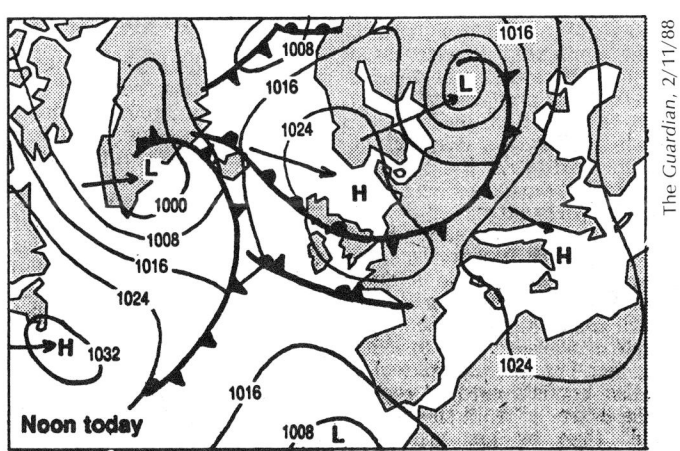

▲ **29.3** *Weather forecast, 2 November*

2. EUROPE

30. BREAK A LEG!
Ski resorts and ski reports

St Johann im Pongau is a small ski resort near Salzburg in Austria.

▲ **30.1** *A hotel in St Johann im Pongau in winter*

▲ **30.2** *The same hotel in St Johann im Pongau in summer*

1 1. Look at photographs **30.1** and **30.2**, which show the same place in summer and winter. You can see some big changes in use between the seasons. List the changes.

2. Copy table **30.4** and place the activities shown in **30.3** under the right headings.

2 During the winter months newspapers in Britain give ski reports for popular resorts. The reports normally give an account of:
a) the depth of snow
b) the state of the piste (ski run)
c) the conditions for off-piste skiing
d) the type of snow (powder or ice)
e) the weather conditions.

Map **30.5** shows the ski report for 30 December.

1. Using map **30.5**, write a paragraph describing the skiing conditions at Obergurgl in Austria.

indoor swimming skittle alley
photography
Tennis sightseeing shooting range
squash hang gliding
skiing
sketching (drawing) hiking
tobogganing ice skating

▲ 30.3

Winter	Summer	All year round

▲ 30.4   ▼ 30.5

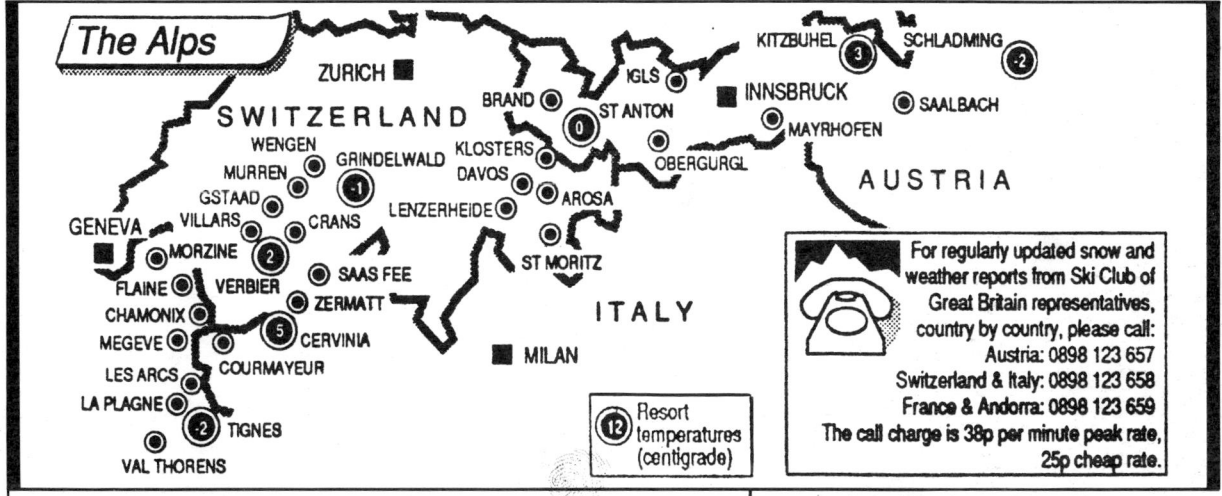

Compiled for the Guardian by the Ski Club of Great Britain.

	Lower slopes (cm)	Upper slopes (cm)	Piste	Off-Piste	COMMENTS
AUSTRIA					
Igls	0	90	Good	Heavy	Good skiing high up
Kitzbühel	15	130	Good	Varied	Flattering pistes and suntans
St Anton	40	240	Good	Spring	Lovely spring snow skiing
Obergurgl	60	85	Worn	Heavy	Good skiing still available
Schladming	9	140	Fair	Heavy	Good skiing above mid lift stations
Saalbach/Hinterglemm	50	160	Fair	Varied	Some pistes becoming worn
FRANCE					
Chamonix	25	120	Fair	Fair	Good sunny skiing in all areas
Flaine	38	86	Fair	Varied	Good skiing above 2000 m
Tignes	55	210	Fair	Varied	Good sunny skiing all over
Val Thorens	15	40	Poor	Poor	Pistes are badly worn
ITALY					
Cervinia	20	140	Fair	Crust	Best on high and north facing slopes
SWITZERLAND					
Crans Montana	29	70	Worn	Varied	Spring like conditions
Davos	50	120	Good	Varied	Superb skiing all areas, well worth a visit
Grindelwald	30	110	Fair	Varied	Still good skiing on upper slopes
Verbier	5	140	Worn	Varied	Best skiing on Mont Fort

65

2. EUROPE

31. COSTA? SI!
Coastal Spain

▲ 31.1 *Spain and the Costas*

Costa Brava lies in the north-east. It means 'the wild coast'. Gerona or Barcelona airports are used to get there. The main resorts are L'Estartit, Calella, Lloret de Mar, Tossa de Mar and Barcelona. The area has sunshine, beautiful seas, lovely beaches and masses of entertainment. This is the place for a lively beach holiday.

Costa Dorada means 'the Golden Coast'. It has long sandy beaches, quaint old towns and fishing villages. Tarragona is an ancient city dating back to Roman times. Costa Dorada uses Gerona airport. Its main resorts are Salou and Malgrat de Mar.

Costa del Sol is steeped in Spanish traditions: flamenco dancing and sea food. It has a rugged coastline, small coves and whitewashed hamlets. It's in the region of Andalusia. The main resorts are Torremolinos and Nerja, served by Malaga airport.

Costa Blanca – the white coast – is the favourite sunspot. It attracts many people because of the blue skies, beaches and non-stop action. There is a good choice of resorts from Alicante, Benidorm and Villajoyosa to Denia. This region is reached by Alicante airport.

Costa del Azahar: the orange blossom coast. This coast is the most varied. There's the ancient town of Peniscola, the seaside resort of Torreblanca and the picturesque, rocky mountains and sandy beaches of Oropesa. The Costa del Azahar uses Reus airport.

▲ 31.2

1 1. Two students are spending the summer exploring Europe by bicycle. They will travel from the Costa Brava in the north to the Costa del Sol in the south. Using map **31.1**, rearrange their stopover places in a sensible order to avoid too much cycling in hot weather.

   Tarragona   Alicante   Valencia   Almeria
   Barcelona   Malaga

  2. Using map **31.1**, calculate how far it is by road from
     a) Barcelona to Valencia
     b) Cadiz to Malaga.

2 Table **31.3** shows the names of several hotels, and the resorts they are in. Copy out the table and using the information in **31.2**, fill in the name of the Costa the resort is on, and which airport a visitor would use.

Hotel	Costa	Airport
Hostal Picasso (Almeria)		
Hostal Expresso (Lloret de Mar)		
Pension La Marina (Salou)		
Hostal Juan (Torremolinos)		
Pension El Pino (Benidorm)		
Hostal Bona Vista (Torreblanca)		

▲ 31.3

Over to you . . .

Not everyone would wish to travel by bicycle in Spain in the summer. Using the information in Units 28, 29, 31 and 32, decide what sort of Spanish holiday you would like. You can plan your holiday using travel brochures or an atlas.

2. EUROPE

32. OLD AND NEW:
Spanish holidays

1 Photos **32.1** and **32.2** show two different attractions of a Spanish holiday.

▲ **32.1** *Historic Cordoba*

◀ **32.2** *Modern Marbella*

Make sketches of the scenes in the photographs and label the attractions of the two places, bringing out the differences between them.

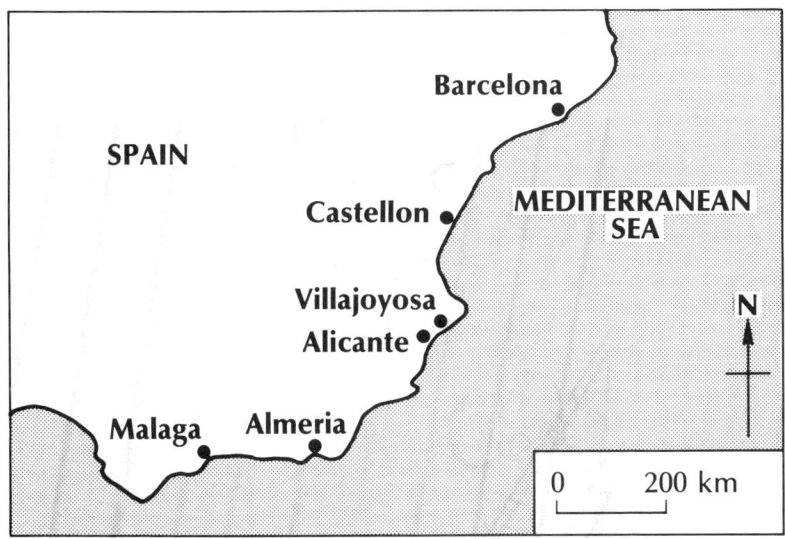

▲ **32.3** *South-east Spain*

2 Look at map **32.3**.

At the end of July, Anne and David Fleming fly to Alicante to stay at the Hostal Siesta, near Villajoyosa. It is fiesta week. They join in many activities: water sports, street market shopping, flamenco and disco dancing.

They also have two free days, including an overnight stop away from Villajoyosa. Anne wants to visit Castellon, a historic town. David intends to go to Malaga, the birthplace of Picasso.

How can they organise their time? Will they be able to do both trips together, or will they have to do them separately?

Millions of people visit coastal Spain every year. This causes problems both for local people and for tourists. For example, there can be major delays at airports at the beginning and end of the most busy holiday weeks.

Can you think of any other problems tourists cause?

Worksheet 27 examines how people are tackling one major problem in the Mediterranean area.

69

2. EUROPE

33. ALL ROADS LEAD TO ROME:
Main roads in Italy

1 Map **33.1** shows the outline of most of Italy. The main towns are marked by their initial letters. Using table **33.2** work out the name that goes with each initial letter. Then, on your own copy of the map, write in the names.

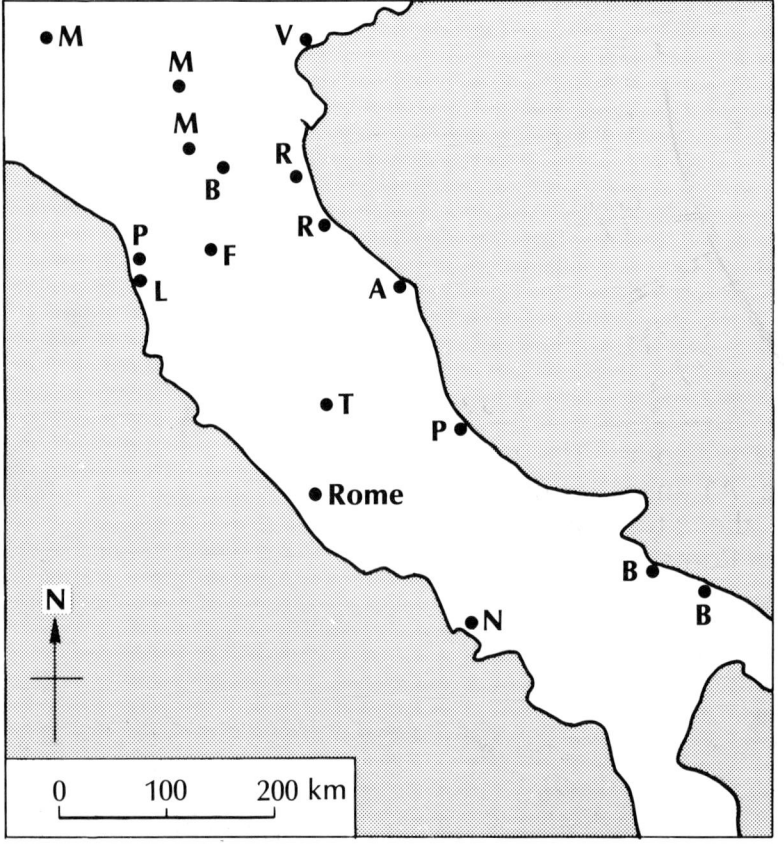

City	Distance from Rome (km)
Rimini	330
Leghorn (Livorno)	317
Pisa	336
Milan (Milano)	575
Florence (Firenze)	278
Venice (Venezia)	539
Mantua (Mantova)	477
Modena	406
Ravenna	373
Ancona	291
Terni	97
Bologna	380
Pescara	235
Barletta	430
Bari	467
Naples (Napoli)	217

▲ 33.2

◀ 33.1 *Major towns in part of Italy*

2 Rome once ruled most of Europe. One trademark of the Roman Empire was its long straight roads, connecting together important centres. Italy still has a good road network connecting the rest of the country to Rome.

Using an atlas, or a road map of Italy, find out which cities are linked by motorways. Then, on your own copy of map **33.1**, draw straight lines between those cities. This forms a **topological** map of the motorway network.

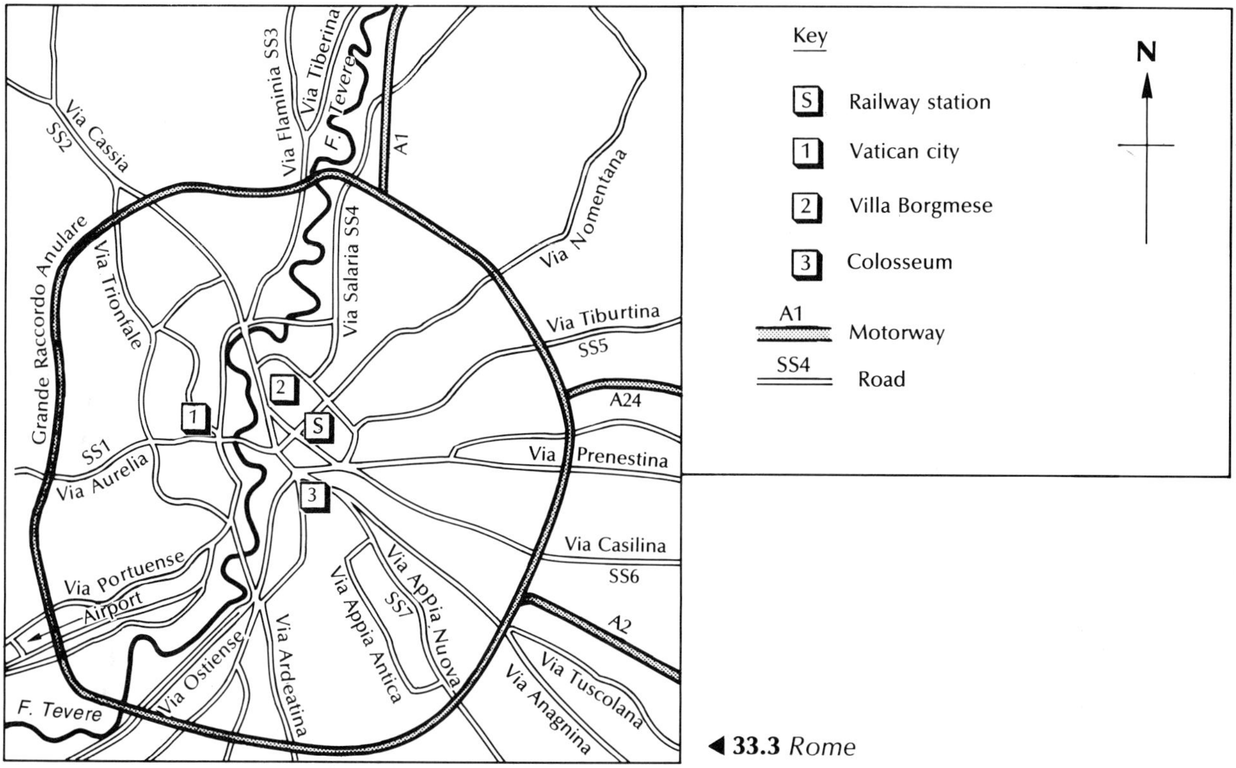

◀ 33.3 Rome

Map **33.3** shows the central area of Rome. The map shows the motorways (Autostrade: A1 and A2) and the ordinary roads (Via) meeting in the city. Roads and railways from all over Italy meet in Rome.

The railway is not marked but the station is. Three of the most important historical sites have also been marked. The River Tiber (Tevere) goes through the city.

Map **33.3** also shows the Great Ring Road (Grande Raccordo Anulare), which keeps traffic out of the centre of Rome where the streets are crowded and narrow. What are the advantages of a city with fewer cars? Worksheet 33 looks at some problems faced by transport planners in cities and some solutions they have proposed.

The next step . . .

Choose four of the towns marked on map **33.1** and find out, from tourist brochures, why people might be interested in visiting them.

71

2. EUROPE

34. GRASPING GREEK GRAPHS:
Tourism in Greece

1 Graph **34.1** is a **bar graph** showing the estimated numbers of tourists from various countries arriving in Greece in 1988.

1. From which country did most visitors come?
2. From which countries did least come?
3. Which five countries were providing most visitors to Greece? Put them in order, number 1 being the country that sends the most. This is called ranking.
4. Make a list of reasons why Greece is popular with people from those countries. For example, think about weather and distances. Can you think of any other reasons?

▼ **34.1** *Tourist arrivals by nationality, 1988*

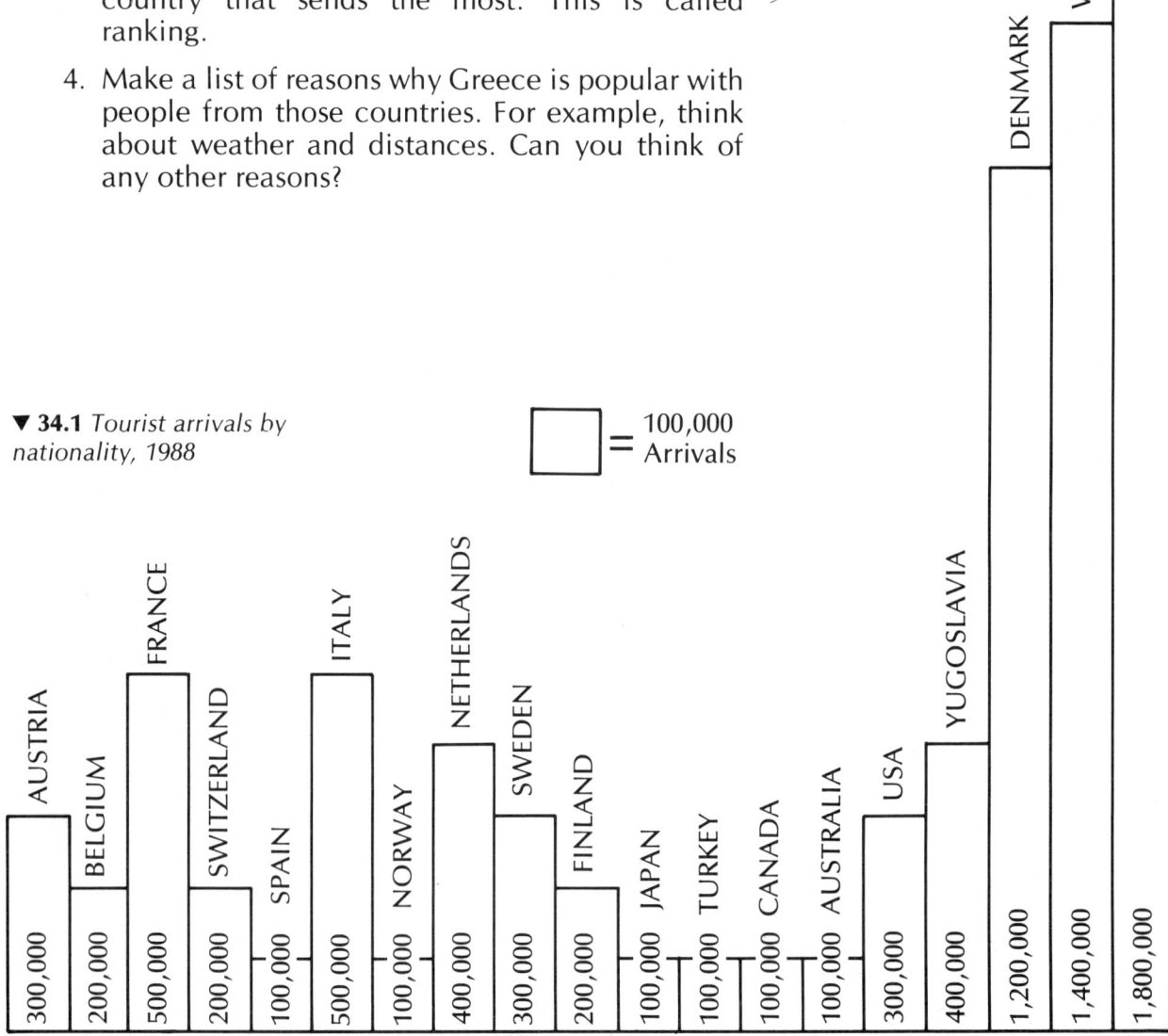

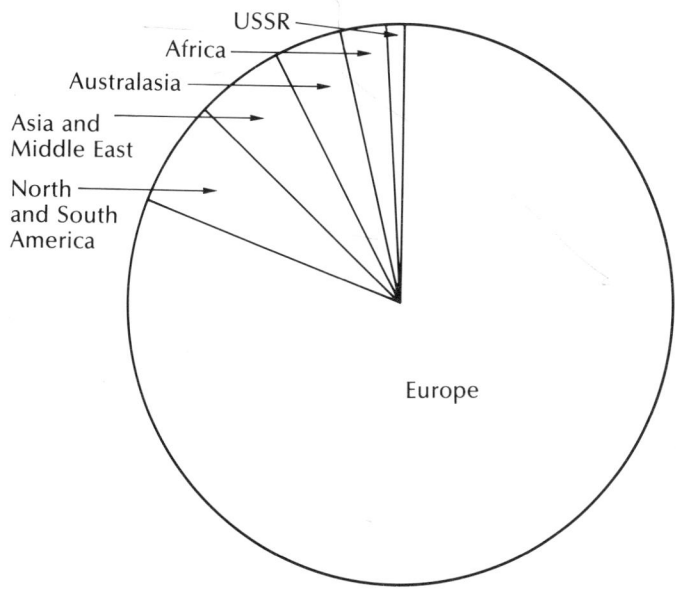

◀ **34.2** *Tourist arrivals from all countries, 1985*

2 Chart **34.2** is a **pie chart** showing tourist arrivals in Greece in 1985. It groups visitors according to which area or continent they come from.

1. Why did the majority of visitors come from Europe?
2. Can you work out why Greece is so attractive to Americans?

3
1. Construct your own bar graph to show the information in table **34.3**. Use 1cm to represent 100,000 tourists. Round the numbers to the nearest 100,000.
2. Your bar graph is on the same scale as graph **34.1**. Compare the two graphs. Did more tourists travel to Greece from any of these countries in 1988 than arrived in 1986? Which countries?
3. Which country shows no increase?

Country of origin	Number of tourists
Austria	293,000
Belgium	118,000
Netherlands	330,000
USA	204,000

▲ **34.3** *Tourist arrivals by nationality, 1986*

And so to . . .

Watch or listen to the news and look at newspapers for one week. Make a note every time one of the following countries is mentioned: France, Greece, Italy, Norway, Spain, Sweden, Switzerland.

Put your results into a graph. If one country has more mentions than the others try to explain the reason for this.

2. EUROPE

35. AWAY FROM IT ALL:
The Greek Islands

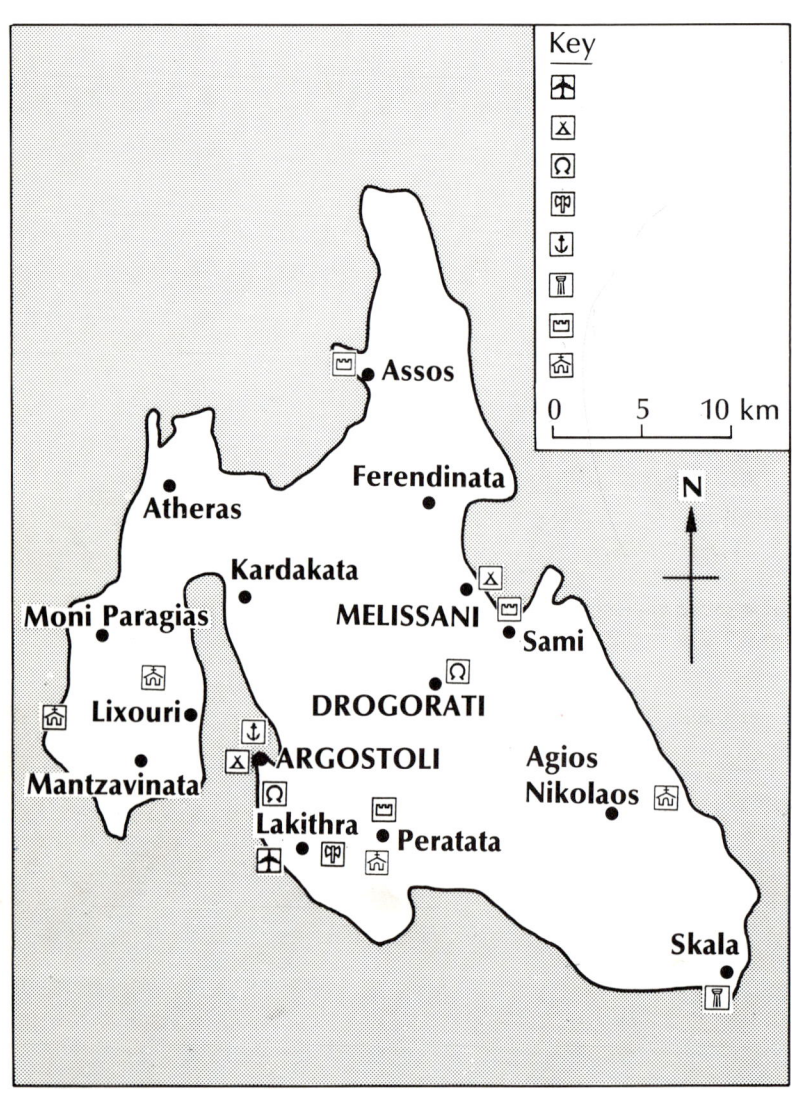

▲ 35.1 *Cephalonia*

Ian and Lesley Miller are going to visit the Greek island of Cephalonia for the summer holidays. The tourist office has given them map **35.1** and a description of the island (**35.2**).

1 The map has no key. Can you work out what the symbols mean? If you read the description and match it to the map, you can work out the key.

> **Cephalonia** is the largest island in the Ionian Sea. It is a beautiful holiday island. Visitors come to sunbathe on the splendid beaches, cruise on yachts around its shores and visit the many historic sites.
>
> Much of the old town of Argostoli was destroyed by an earthquake in 1953. Near the town you can camp and swim. The town has a yacht supply centre.
>
> The beaches near Lixouri are among the best on the island. To the west of Lixouri is the monastery of Panagias. Among the other monasteries found on the island is one south of Peratata.
>
> Assos is a charming village with a famous picturesque castle, built to protect the island from pirates.
>
> Skala, in the extreme south, has good beaches and ruins dating back to the third centry BC. It is an important archeological site. Another historic site is Stavros, which has prehistoric remains.
>
> There are interesting caves at Drogorati with stalagmites and stalagtites.

▲ 35.2

2 Using map **35.1** and your key, answer the following questions in complete sentences.

1. Apart from the campsite near Argostoli, where else can you find a campsite?
2. Apart from Assos, where can you find castles?
3. What type of historic site is found south of Lakithra?
4. In which part of the island would you arrive by plane (north, south, east or west)?
5. What else would you like to know about the island which is not shown on the map?

A testing activity . . .

In pairs, use Worksheet 35 or the key of an Ordnance Survey 1:50,000 map to test each other on the symbols used in Ordnance Survey maps. How many can you recognise?

2. EUROPE

36. EURO TOUR:
The European Community

The European Community was formed in 1957, with six member countries. Since then more countries have joined. In 1973 there were nine countries, and by 1986 there were twelve. The United Kingdom joined in 1973. The European Community plans to remove the customs barriers between the countries by 1 January 1993.

The twelve present member countries of the European Community (EC) are shaded on the map of Europe, map **36.1**. They are the United Kingdom, Eire, Spain, Portugal, Greece, France, Italy, Denmark, Belgium, Netherlands, Luxembourg and West Germany.

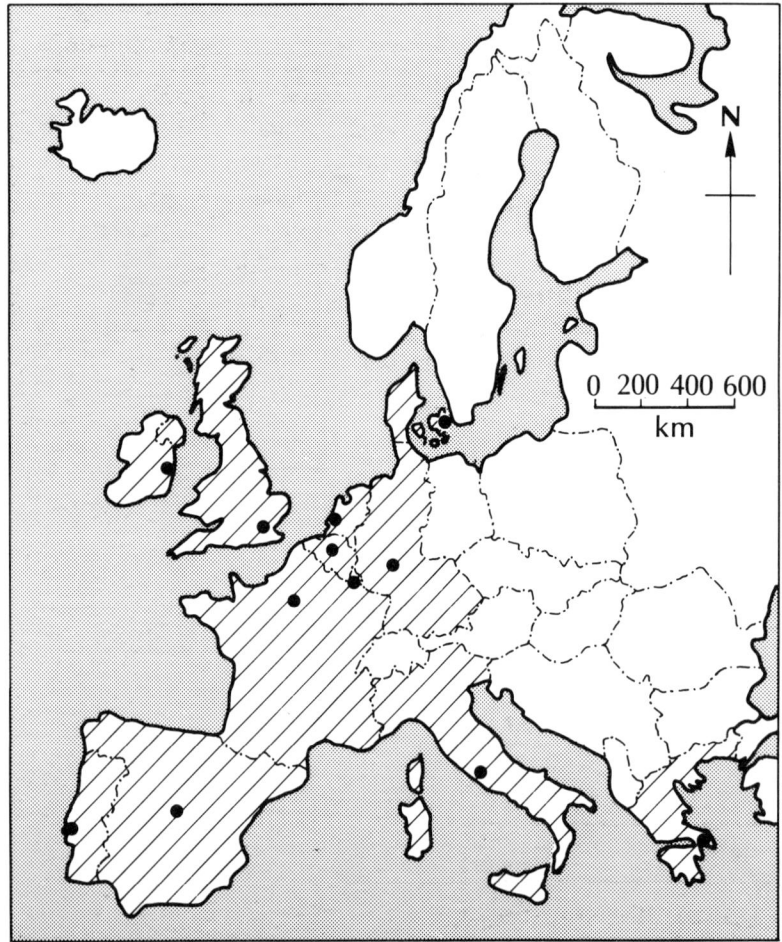

▲ **36.1** *Countries of the European Community*

1 1. Use an atlas to identify the countries and, using a coloured pen, mark the names on your own copy of the map.

2. Dots mark the location of the twelve capital cities. Match the names of the cities in box **36.2** to the countries and mark them on your map.

2 The countries are very varied in their scenery, their climate and how they use their land.

Table **36.3** shows how land is used in the EC as a whole.

1. Draw a pie chart to show these figures. Remember that the whole circle is 360 degrees, so 58% = 210 degrees, 9% = 32 degrees.
2. What does the pie chart show as the main land use in Europe?
3. What types of land use are there in your home area?

3 Many countries in Europe are not part of the European Community. Look at a map of Europe in an atlas.

1. On your own copy of map **36.1**, in a different colour from the one you used to mark the EC countries, mark the following countries:
East Germany   Poland   Norway   Sweden
Austria   Romania   Bulgaria   Yugoslavia
Finland   Switzerland   Albania   Hungary
Iceland   Czechoslovakia

2. Use your atlas to mark on your copy of the map these important European cities:
a) Zurich – a famous financial centre
b) Hamburg and Rotterdam – two big European ports
c) Berlin – jointly owned by East and West Germany

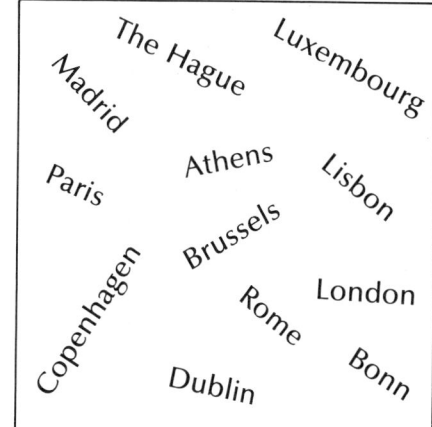

▲ **36.2**

Land use	Percentage of the whole
Agricultural land	58%
Wooded land	22%
Built up and industrial land	9%
Inland waters	2%
Other (including mountain peaks)	9%

▲ **36.3**

More art work . . .

Make a poster showing the flags of the member countries of the European Community.

77

3. NORTH AMERICA

37. NEW YORK, NEW YORK!
Manhattan Island

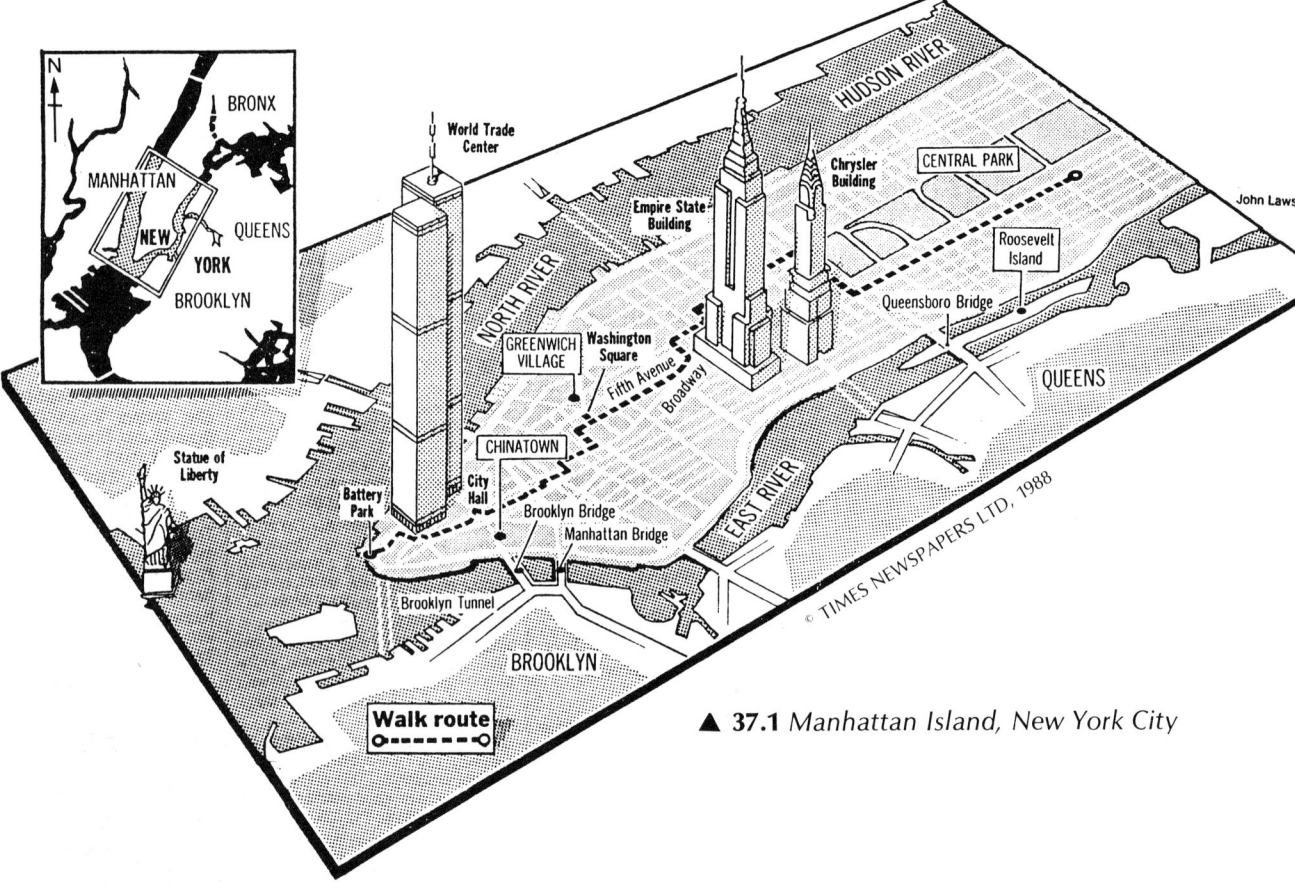

▲ 37.1 *Manhattan Island, New York City*

Map **37.1** is a diagrammatic map of part of the centre of New York. It shows Manhattan Island and its landmarks.

The World Trade Center is one of the tallest buildings in the world. Fifth Avenue is a famous shopping street. Broadway is the area for theatres and cinemas. The open sea is past the Statue of Liberty in the south-west of the map.

1
1. The map shows two ways of crossing the river to Manhattan. What are they?
2. How can you tell from the street pattern that Manhattan was a planned area?

3. Along the banks of the North River and the Hudson River you can see the piers and wharves of the old port, where the boats dock. Why do you think there are very few docks on the East River?

2 A planned walk is shown on map **37.1**.

1. If you start your walk from the north-east end, by Central Park, what do you see if you look south-west? Is it a help to the walker to be able to see the shape of buildings on the map?

2. At the south-western end of the walk there is a famous view. What can you see?

3 The walk is planned to show you some of the features of Manhattan. As well as the buildings, there are districts marked on the map which are near the walk route. China Town is an interesting and lively area famous for its Chinese shops and restaurants. Greenwich Village is well known as a meeting place for artists and musicians.

1. Which of these can you visit at the same time as Washington Square?

2. The map also shows the names of areas beyond the Island of Manhattan. What is the area to the north-east of Manhattan called?

3. Find out how Roosevelt Island got its name.

4. In order to plan another walk using map **37.1** there is something else you would need to know about the map. What is it?

▲ *Manhattan skyline*

How do you see it . . . ?

Many television programmes and films have been made about New York. They give us a perception (an idea) of what the place is like. What is your perception of New York City? Write a paragraph about it.

3. NORTH AMERICA

38. GOING WEST:
Flying to the USA

If you fly to the USA, you will usually have a choice of airline and airport. You can also choose between a direct flight or one with stops.

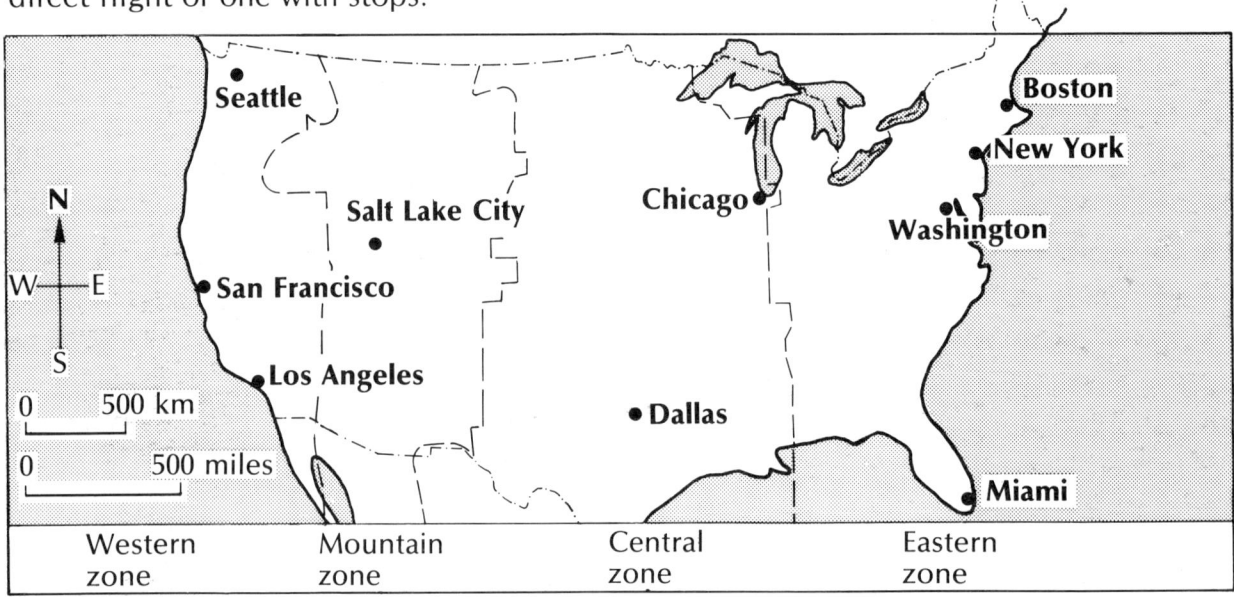

▲ 38.1 *Location of major cities in the USA*

	Outward bound from Heathrow				Outward bound from Gatwick			
	Flight No.	Depart	Arrive	Routing	Flight No.	Depart	Arrive	Routing
Boston	TW 753	11.00	13.15	Non-stop	NW 49	11.20	12.30	Non-stop
Chicago	TW 771	11.30	14.03	Non-stop	NW 49	11.20	16.40	Boston
Dallas	TW 01	13.30	20.55	New York	AA 51	11.55	14.55	Non-stop
Los Angeles	TW 761	12.25	15.25	Non-stop	BR 223	12.45	16.00	Non-stop
Miami	TW 701	13.30	22.12	New York	AA 51	11.55	20.59	Dallas
New York	TW 703	12.00	14.40	Non-stop	BR 267	11.30	14.25	Non-stop
Salt Lake City	—	—	—	—	AA 79	14.25	20.21	Dallas
San Francisco	TW 761	12.25	18.42	Los Angeles	AA 737	11.55	17.43	Dallas
Seattle	TW 705	13.30	21.45	New York	NW 45	13.35	20.38	Minneapolis
Washington	TW 703	12.00	17.56	New York	—	—	—	—

▲ 38.2

Map **38.1** shows ten locations in the United States. Table **38.2** shows a tour operator's flight timetables to the USA from London's first airport, Heathrow, and London's second airport, Gatwick.

1 Using the tour operator's timetable, table **38.2**, work out answers to the following questions:

1. To which American airport does the operator not offer flights from Gatwick?
2. Which number flight from Gatwick calls at Boston?
3. If I take flight TW761 from Heathrow what are my possible destinations?
4. A tourist has tickets for a 13.30 flight to Dallas. Which airport must he fly from?
5. Which airport must I fly from to arrive in Boston as early as possible in the day?

The departure and arrival times shown in timetable **38.2** are rather misleading because of the time change as you travel west from Britain.

Time is calculated relative to the standard or **Mean** time at Greenwich in London, which is at 0 degrees **longitude**. Because, as the earth spins, the sun rises in the east, everywhere west of Greenwich up to 180 degrees longitude (half-way round the world) has sunrise later than Britain. So if a place is 90 degrees west, a quarter of the way round the world, it will be quarter of a day behind London: that is it will only be 6 a.m. there when it is 12 noon in Greenwich.

There are four **time zones** in the USA. The Eastern zone is five hours behind London, the Central zone six hours, the Rocky Mountains seven hours and the Western zone eight hours behind London. If you fly to Boston or New York from London you must add five hours to the arrival time given in the timetable to work out how many hours you are actually in the air.

2
1. Calculate the total travelling time if you take a) flight TW701 from Heathrow to Miami, b) flight TW761 from Heathrow to San Francisco.
2. Which of the flights on the timetable would involve the shortest travelling time?

3. NORTH AMERICA

39. CROSSING THE CONTINENT:
Travel in the USA

There are many ways to travel around the USA. Greyhound buses are a good way to see the country. Some of the trains also have special viewing carriages. Because of the long distances between towns, many people travel by air.

Table **39.1** shows distances by air between US cities. To work out the distance between two places, find one city on the horizontal axis, and the other on the vertical axis. Read across from one and down from the other. The distance is the number where the two lines meet. You can check your answer by finding the places again on the opposite axes. Dallas to Chicago has been shown for you.

1
1. Which two cities are the furthest apart by air?
2. Which two cities are closest?
3. Which town is 1092 miles from New York?
4. How far would you have travelled in total if you went from New York to Boston, from there to Chicago and from there to Seattle?

Approximate distances in miles, by air	Boston	Chicago	Dallas	Los Angeles	Miami	New York	Salt Lake City	San Francisco	Seattle	Washington
Boston		851	1551	2596	1255	188	2099	2699	2493	393
Chicago	851		803	1745	1188	713	1260	1858	1737	597
Dallas	1551	803		1240	1111	1374	999	1483	1681	1185
Los Angeles	2596	1745	1240		2339	2451	579	347	959	2300
Miami	1255	1188	1111	2339		1092	2089	2594	2734	923
New York	188	713	1374	2451	1092		1972	2568	2408	205
Salt Lake City	2099	1260	999	579	2089	1972		600	701	1848
San Francisco	2699	1858	1483	347	2594	2568	600		678	2442
Seattle	2493	1737	1681	959	2734	2408	701	678		2329
Washington DC	393	597	1185	2300	923	205	1848	2442	2329	

▲ 39.1

How far . . .

Roads and railways are usually shown on atlas maps. Using a piece of string and the scale on the atlas, work out if the places in table **39.1** are a similar distance or much further apart by rail or road than by air.

Note: Table **39.1** shows distances in miles not kilometres. Check that the scale on the atlas is also in miles.

3. NORTH AMERICA

40. IN THE PICTURE:
Tourist centres in the USA

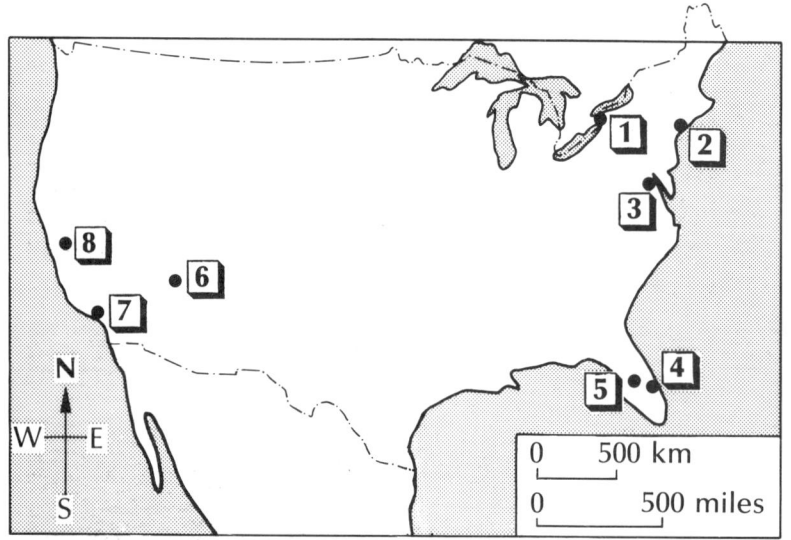
▲ 40.1 Tourist centres in the USA

▲ Statue of Liberty, New York

▲ Capitol Building, Washington DC

▲ Niagara Falls, between Lakes Erie and Ontario

▲ Californian redwoods, Yosemite

▲ The White House, Washington DC, home of the US President

▲ Rocket launch at Cape Canaveral

▲ Grand Canyon, Arizona

The photographs show just a few of the places people visit in the United States of America.

1. Look at map **40.1**, the outline map of the USA. The numbered dots represent the locations where the photographs were taken (two were taken in the same place). Use an atlas to match the names to the numbers on the map.

2. Find out from an encyclopedia whether these statements are true or false:
   1. The area of the USA is 22.4 million square kilometres.
   2. The largest city is New York.
   3. The highest mountain is Mount McKinley.
   4. The longest river is the Mississippi–Missouri.
   5. The largest lake is Lake Superior.
   6. The highest waterfall is Yosemite.

▲ Whale at 'Sea World', Orlando

▲ Los Angeles – home of the stars

Further Tasks... on images of the United States can be found on Worksheet 40.

3. NORTH AMERICA

41. HOT OR COLD? WET OR DRY?
Climate in the USA

The graphs in table **41.1** show the climate of four cities across the United States of America. The locations of the four cities are shown on map **41.2**.

They are all at approximately the same **latitude** – 33–38 degrees north of the Equator. They are at different **longitudes**. These places are all west of Greenwich. As you can see from the map, Los Angeles is the furthest west. Although they are all about the same distance from the Equator, they have different patterns of rainfall and temperature.

▼ 41.1

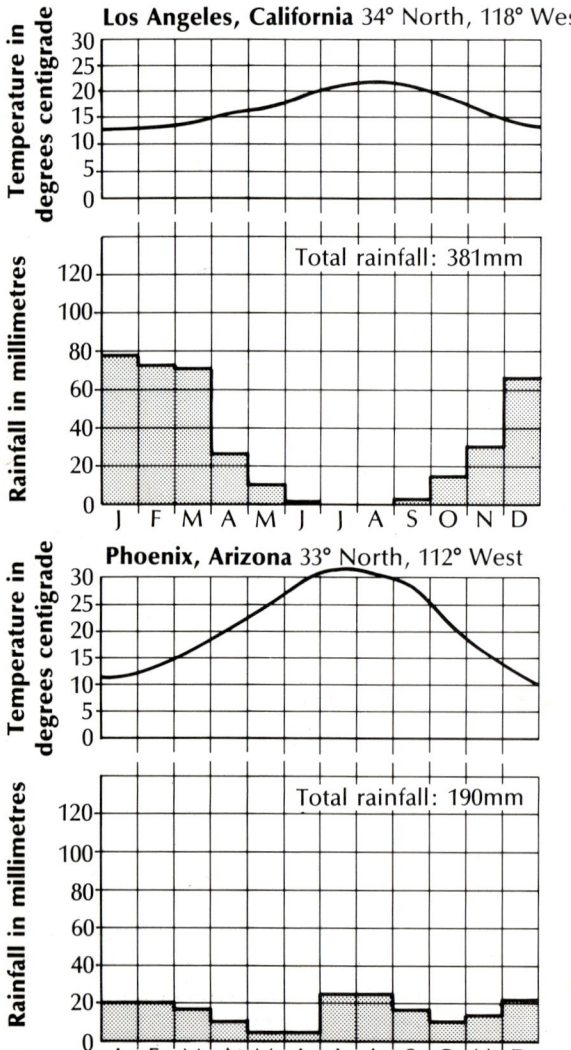
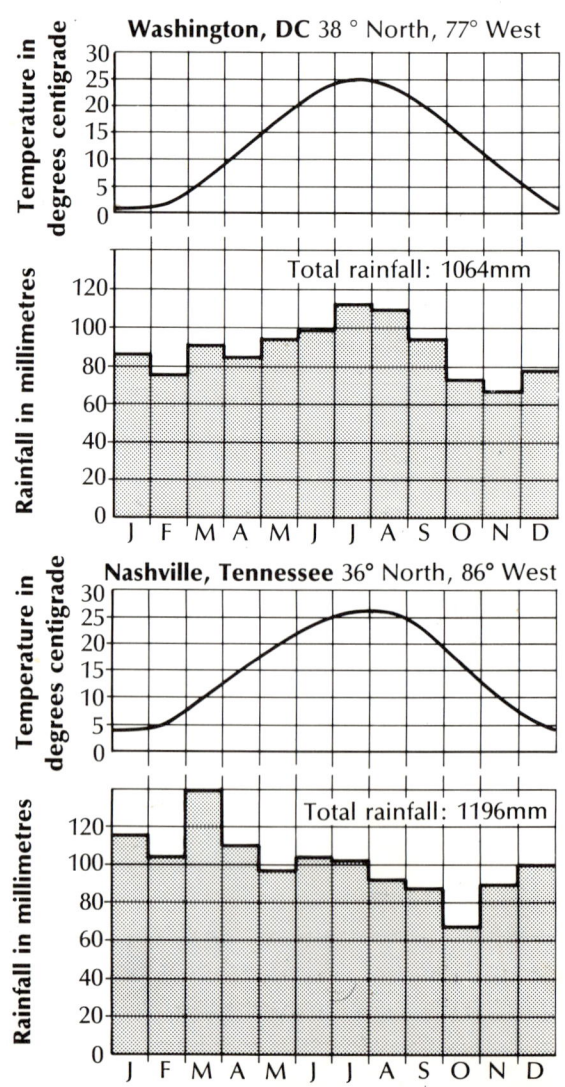

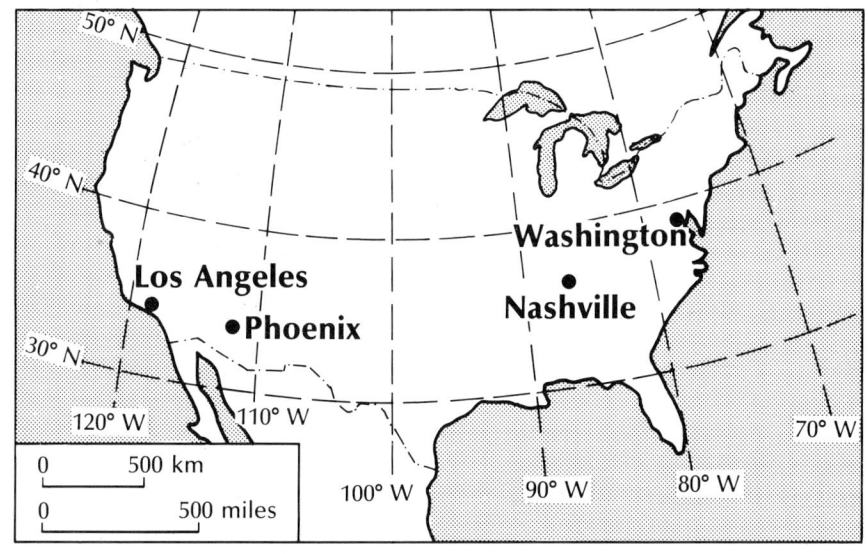

◀ 41.2 *The USA*

1
1. Which place is the wettest?
2. Which place is the driest?
3. Los Angeles has a rainfall pattern that suits tourists but does not suit farmers. Can you explain why?
4. The cities of Washington and Nashville are only 900 km apart. They have similar climates. Which are the warmest months for each city? Which are the coolest? Which are the driest months?
5. Which climate has the greatest temperature range (the difference between highest and lowest temperature)?

2 Phoenix has a dry climate because it does not receive wet winds from the sea. Diagram **41.3** explains why it is that the hottest months are also the wettest. The reason is **convectional rainfall**.

1. Which two months are both hottest and wettest in Phoenix?
2. In Britain most of our rain does not come from convection currents. Why?

Find out . . .

In a Geography book, find a section describing how rainfall occurs. What other types of rainfall are there apart from convectional rainfall?

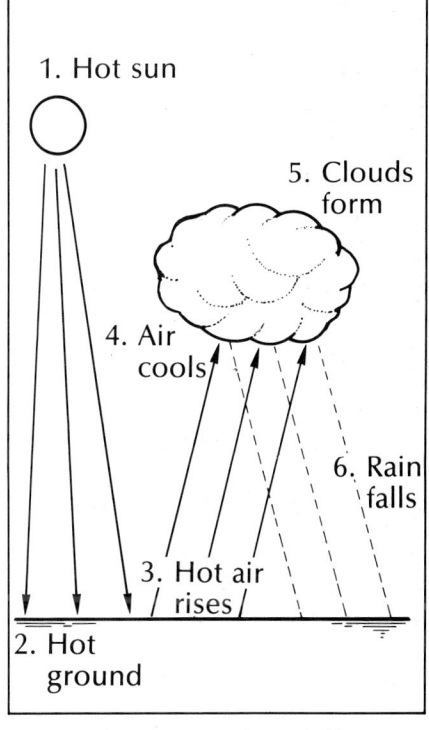

▲ 41.3 *Convectional rainfall. The hot sun warms the ground and warm air currents rise. As they rise they get cooler and the moisture in the air condenses to form clouds. If enough moisture collects in the clouds they produce rainfall.*

3. NORTH AMERICA

42. CANADA CALLING:
Canada

Canada covers a bigger land area than its neighbour the United States – but it has many less people. The large central area in particular is very **sparsely populated**.

1 The crossword grid **42.1** will help you find out things about Canada. Some of the answers can be found in an atlas, but you will have to hunt for others. The number in brackets after each clue tells you how many letters there are in the answer.

◀ 42.1

Clues Across

3. A town on the west coast, near Vancouver. Also the name of an English queen. (8)

4. Canada is divided into areas called provinces. This province contains many mountains. (7)

10. A large town on the St Lawrence estuary in eastern Canada. (8)

11. A French word meaning 'of the' – part of the name of the northern town Fond .. Lac. (2)

12. A large lake on the border of the USA and Canada which flows into the Niagara Falls. (4)

13. and 16 Down. A line of latitude (66 degrees) in the cold north. (6, 6)

88

17. The first part of the name of several towns in the mid-west. It reminds us that these towns were originally bases for soldiers fighting wars against the local Indian tribes. (4)
19. See 2 Down.
22. A European language spoken by many people in Eastern Canada. (6)
23. An important fuel drilled in Alberta, and used to make petrol. (3)

Clues Down

1. The emblem of Canada. The sap of the tree is used to make syrup for waffles. (5, 4)
2. and 19 across. One raw material used for making steel. It is mined in Labrador. (4, 3)
3. The main town in western Canada. (9)
5. An area of sea, as in Hudson – – – . (3)
6. The capital of Canada. (6)
7. A province and city in eastern Canada. (6)
8. The very valuable metal found in Canada's mountains, which attracted people to explore remote areas. (4)
9. The cereal crop grown in the Prairies of Saskatchewan. (5)
14. The – – – – – Mountains: the highest mountains in Canada. (5)
15. North is usually at the – – – of the map. (3)
16. See 13 across.
18. The St Lawrence is a – – – – – . (5)
20. The – – – – coast of Canada is nearest to Europe. (4)
21. The abbreviation for British Columbia. (2)

Over to you . . .
Make up your own crossword using place names in North America. An atlas will help.

Further Tasks... on Canada's large empty areas can be found on Worksheet 42.

4. THE SOUTHERN CONTINENTS AND ASIA

43. DOWN UNDER:
Images of Australia

People have many different images of Australia.

1 Do you recognise any of these?

▲ Early settlement at Botany Bay

▲ The original inhabitants of Australia

▲ The 'Akubra' hat which keeps off the sun and rain and has additions to keep off flies

▲ The wildlife of the outback

▲ The 'tinny'

▲ An animal introduced from Britain, which became a pest, eating the grass farm animals needed

90

▲ Farming in the outback on large areas of poor grassland and eucalyptus scrub: the farms are called 'stations'

▲ The biggest city, with an Opera House built to represent the sails of boats in the harbour

▲ The nearby Pacific with 'breakers' ideal for this sport

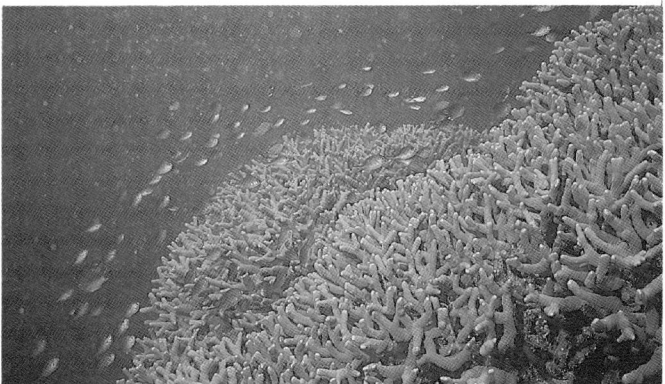
▲ The Great Barrier Reef – with millions of fish swimming in warm coral waters

These might be the most common images. But they give only a selected impression of a very large and varied country where:

- wine production is as important as brewing beer
- growing tropical fruits is almost as important as keeping sheep
- iron ore, uranium and gold are mined
- industry is as important as farming.

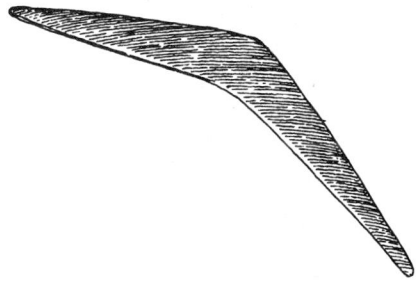
▲ The weapon some native aborigines still use to kill animals for food

More . . .

From the Geography or Travel sections in a library, find books on Australia. Use them to write an essay called: 'The places I would like to visit in Australia'.

91

4. THE SOUTHERN CONTINENTS AND ASIA

44. NEIGHBOURS?
Distances in Australia

◀ 44.1 *Major cities and roads in Australia*

Map **44.1** shows the major cities and main roads in Australia. From the scale of the map you can see that the country is very large and there are long distances between the main areas where people live.

1 Use the scale and a piece of string to work out the distances by road between:
a) Adelaide and Darwin
b) Perth and Sydney.

2 Some of the roads marked on the map are dirt roads. Although they are main roads, they do not have an asphalt surface. It is often better, unless you are moving heavy loads, to fly rather than drive. This also avoids the expense of overnight stops.

Including checking-in time and unloading, you must allow about two hours to fly from Brisbane to Sydney and about one hour from Melbourne to Sydney.

1. If a family of tourists drive approximately 480 kilometres in a day, how long will it take them to drive between these cities?

2. The family decide to drive rather than fly. What are the advantages and disadvantages of doing this?

3 1. On your own copy of map **44.1** draw in the direct air routes between all the main cities.

Flying distances in Australia are much shorter than road distances. The differences are caused by difficult conditions in the centre and north of the country which prevent the roads taking a direct route.

2. Work out the difference between road and air distances from:
a) Brisbane to Darwin
b) Brisbane to Perth.

4 1. Find out from an atlas which cities in Australia have more than 1 million people, and which have more than ½ million. Mark them on your own copy of map **44.1**.

2. Most people in Australia live in cities by the coast. Why do you think this is?

3. Using an atlas and your own copy of the map, shade three types of area: deserts, mountains and tropical rainforests. Use a different colour for each of the three. Include the Nullarbor Plain in the south, which is also a desert. The name means 'no trees'.

You will see that although Australia is a very large country, only small areas are easy to live in. Despite this, before the arrival of the Europeans in Australia thousands of aborigines lived successfully in the very difficult desert environment.

Carry on . . .

Find out about:
a) Australia's Flying Doctor service
b) school by radio.

You will find information about these services in library books about Australia.

Why do you think these services are needed in some parts of the country?

4. THE SOUTHERN CONTINENTS AND ASIA

45. BLACK GOLD:
Oil in the Middle East

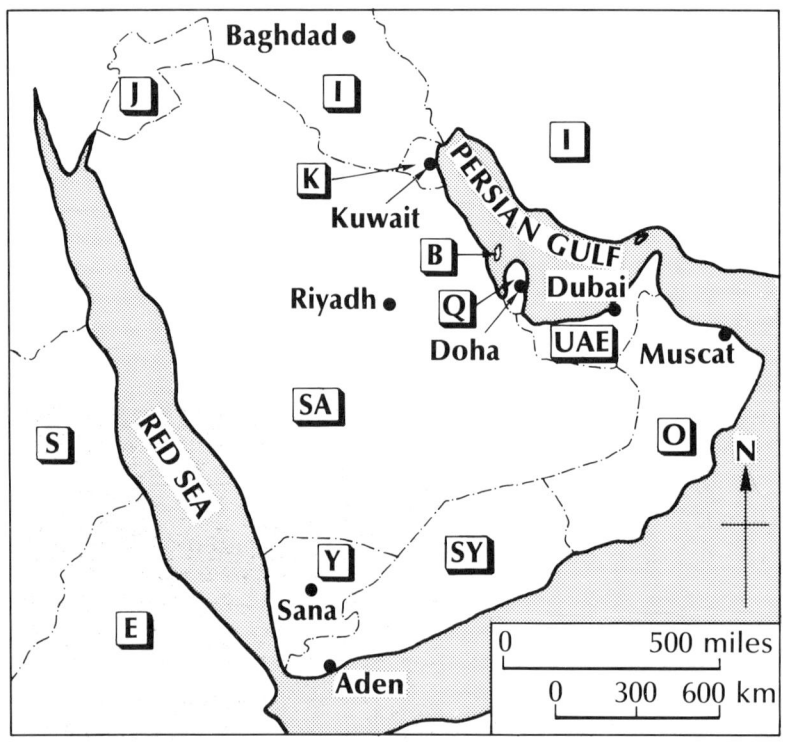

▲ 45.1 *The Middle East*

Map **45.1** shows the area of the Middle East around the Persian Gulf. This is the most important part of the world for oil production.

Before oil was discovered there, most of the countries were desert areas. They had low **Gross National Products**. The Gross National Product or GNP of a country is the total value of all the goods and services produced by the country in a year. This total is usually divided by the number of people in the country to give the GNP **per capita**.

The main type of farming was the herding of animals. Nomads with sheep, goats and camels moved around looking for pasture in the dry lands.

Oil has brought great wealth, especially to the rulers and the people who own the land. This wealth can be seen in a comparison of the Gross National Products of the Middle Eastern countries.

Table **45.2** shows GNPs in United States dollars. (No reliable statistics are available for Iran and Iraq because of the Iran–Iraq war.)

Country	GNP in dollars (1988)
UK	9,110
USA	12,820
Saudi Arabia	12,600
Kuwait	20,900
Egypt	690
Oman	6,090
Yemen	500

▲ 45.2

It is easy to see from this which are the wealthiest and the least wealthy of the Persian Gulf countries. Yemen has very little oil. Kuwait and Saudi Arabia, on the other hand, produce at least nine times as much as they need. Who do they sell their oil to? The world map in Unit 58 will help you to work it out.

1. Look at the Persian Gulf states on map **45.1**. Using an atlas, work out the names of the countries marked by their initial letters, and write them on your own copy of the map.

2. There are many ways the oil-rich states could use their money to improve the lives of people who live there. Look at the following statements and answer the questions that follow in complete sentences.

    1. 'Nearly all food must be imported and the calorie requirements are only just met for most people.' What could be done to change this situation?
    2. 'In the USA there are 600 hospital beds for each 100,000 people, compared with under 200 in Saudi Arabia.' How could oil money be spent here?
    3. 'In 1985, more than eight out of ten people in the USA and the UK could read and write. In Saudi Arabia eight out of ten still can't read or write.' How might more oil money be spent?

▲ *Oil production in the desert*

4. THE SOUTHERN CONTINENTS AND ASIA

46. MEASURING UP:
South America

▲ 46.1 *South America*

▲ 46.2

South America is a large continent made up of large countries, with vast forests, deserts, mountains and big bustling cities.

1 Look at map **46.1**. Count how many countries there are in South America.

2 Each square on map **46.1** represents 40,000 square miles. The grid can be used to work out very roughly the area of a country, as shown in box **46.2**.

1. Use this method to work out the area of the biggest country and one of the smallest countries. Note: The halves or parts of squares are estimated not measured, so your answer may be different to other people's.
2. Great Britain has an area of approximately 89,000 square miles. Is the smallest country you measured smaller or larger than Great Britain?
3. Each square on the grid is 200 miles across. Work out the greatest distance from north to south and from east to west in South America.

3 See how many South American countries you can find in the wordsearch grid **46.3**.

▲ 46.3

Now follow on . . .

Map **46.1** also shows two island groups – one to the north and another to the south-east of South America.

1. See what you can find out about the Falkland Islands, just off the coast of Argentina. What are they famous for? What is their link to the United Kingdom?
2. What can you find out about Trinidad or Barbados in the Caribbean? What links do these islands have to the United Kingdom?
3. Find out what climate each island group has. Which would you prefer to live in? Why?

4. THE SOUTHERN CONTINENTS AND ASIA

47. A GRAND TOUR:
Three weeks in South America

Some tour operators offer wonderful holidays in South America. While it is not possible to travel all round South America in three weeks, the tours aim to show the wonders and the geography of the continent.

▲ 47.1 *Places visited in tour of South America*

Day 1:	The plane lands in Caracas, **Venezuela**.
Day 2:	Tour round Caracas.
Day 3:	Fly to Bogota, the capital of **Colombia**.
Day 4:	Choose to visit either the Gold Museum or the salt mines, or take a cable car up Mount Montserrate.
Day 5:	Fly to Lima in **Peru**. The rest of the day is free.
Day 6:	Tour the sights of Lima – City of Kings.
Day 7:	Early morning transfer to the airport for the flight to Cuzco.
Day 8:	Sightseeing trip round Cuzco, including the ruined Inca fortress.
Day 9:	Travel by narrow gauge railway to Macchu Picchu, Lost City of the Incas.
Day 10:	Explore the Lost City and return to Cuzco.
Day 11:	Take a train across the Andes to Puno.
Day 12:	A trip by hydrofoil across Lake Titicaca and then by bus to La Paz, **Bolivia** the highest city in the world.
Day 13:	A day in La Paz visiting the market and other sites.
Day 14:	Morning transfer to Rio de Janeiro, **Brazil**.
Day 15:	Sightseeing trip round the city, or if the tour is in February, visit the carnival.
Day 16:	South of Rio by road to the uncrowded beaches and the beautiful Corcovado mountains.
Day 17:	Fly from Rio to Manaos in the heart of the Amazon rainforest.
Day 18:	Discover the wonders of the Amazon wildlife from a boat on the River Amazon.
Day 19:	Return south to the futuristic capital of Brazil, Brasilia.
Day 20:	Fly to Rio de Janeiro again, for the flight back to Europe.

This tour can be extended to include **Argentina** and **Chile**. Starting in Buenos Aires, visit the cattle ranches of the Pampas, or rugged Tierra del Fuego in the south. In Chile, visit the deserts, mountains and wine producing areas.

▲ 47.2

1 Look at the itinerary (journey plan), **47.2**. It shows a typical tour in South America.

1. Read the itinerary. Then, on your own copy of map **47.1**, mark the names of the countries mentioned (which are underlined).
2. Using an atlas, match up the names of the towns and cities in the tour (which are in boxes), with the dots on map **47.1**, and mark the names on your own copy of the map.
3. Add the River Amazon and the Andes Mountains.
4. Draw a line on the finished map to show the route of the tour.

2 Four of the cities visited in the three-week tour of South America are listed in table **47.3**.

City	Population
Belo Horizonte	1,814,990
Brasilia	1,202,683
Buenos Aires	2,060,000
Cordoba	1,052,147
Lima	340,339
Rio de Janeiro	5,184,292
Salvador	1,525,831
Santiago	517,473
Sao Paulo	8,584,896
Caracas	1,658,500

▲ 47.3

1. Check which cities are included in the tour. Now rank those four cities in order of size. The largest of the group will be 1 and the smallest 4.
2. Now rank all ten towns in order of size.
3. Does the tour visit the largest and the smallest of the towns on the list?

More . . .

The itinerary in **47.2** lacks the dramatic pictures of the travel brochures. Collect your own pictures to stick round the edge of your map.

4. THE SOUTHERN CONTINENTS AND ASIA

48. ASIAN HEADLINES:
Locations in Asia

Asia is a continent of contrasts. Geographers have divided this varied continent into groups of countries, as you can see in table **48.1**.

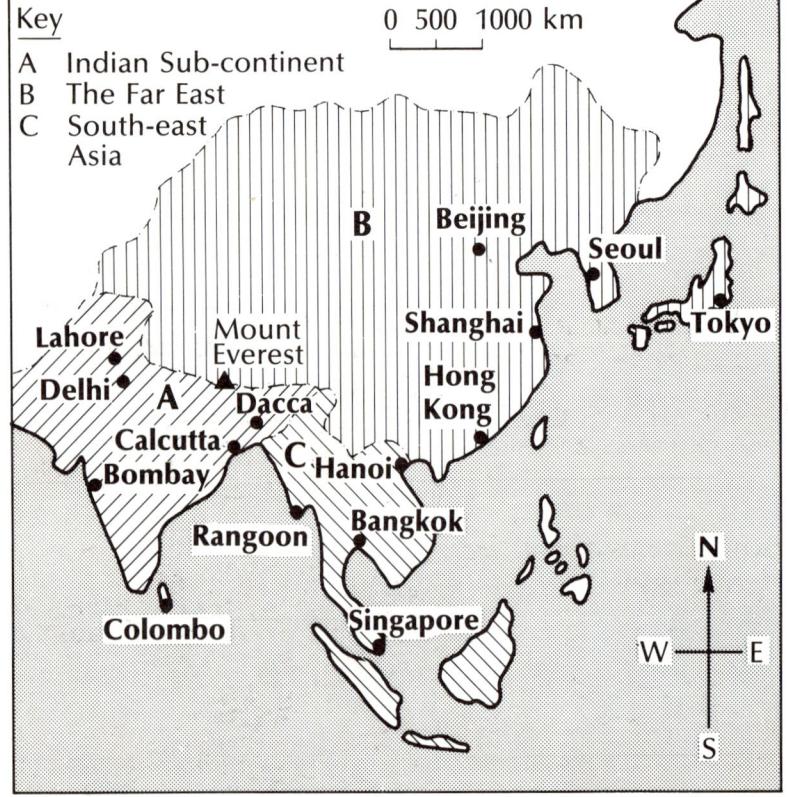

▲ 48.2 *Main areas and cities in Asia*

▲ 48.1

1 Look at map **48.2** of Asia which shows these areas and the main cities. Choose the correct phrase to complete these sentences.

1. Beijing is:
   a) north-west of Hanoi and south of Shanghai
   b) north-east of Calcutta and west of Tokyo
   c) north of Hong Kong and south-east of Dacca.

2. Calcutta is:
   a) north-east of Bombay and west of Lahore
   b) north-west of Colombo and south-west of Delhi
   c) south-west of Shanghai and west of Dacca.

100

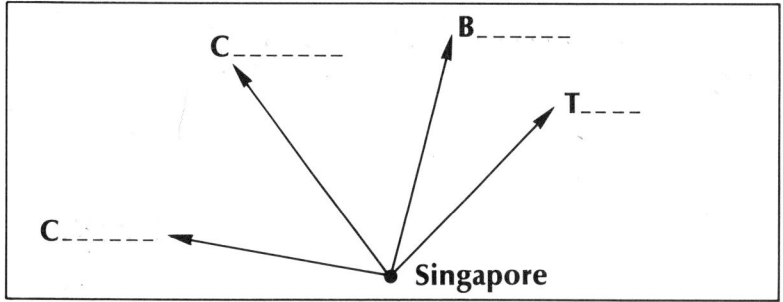

▲ 48.3

2 1. Copy the direction star for Singapore, diagram **48.3**. Compare it with map **48.2** and add the names of the cities which the arrows are pointing towards.

2. Make similar direction stars for Beijing, Hong Kong, Dacca and Bangkok.

3. Use an atlas to find out in which country these three cities are located: Beijing, Dacca, Bangkok.

4. Look in the atlas for Hong Kong and Singapore. They are very small states named after the main town.

3 Often newspaper headlines give us clues about the geography of a country. They may record:
   • the weather
   • imports and exports
   • natural disasters which occur from time to time
   • the physical features of landscapes, such as rivers and highlands.

Look at the Asian headlines in **48.4** and work out which ones refer to each of the following three regions:
a) the Indian sub-continent
b) South-east Asia
c) the Far East.

Look out . . .

Look for your own newspaper headlines about the countries in this unit, and make a collage of them. This activity may take you quite a long time to complete.

▲ 48.4

101

4. THE SOUTHERN CONTINENTS AND ASIA

49. JAPAN BY AIR:
Locations in Japan

Japan is made up of four large islands (altogether nearly 2000 km long) and several smaller islands to the southwest called the Ryukyu Islands. The islands are very mountainous and the most convenient way to travel between cities is by air.

There are two airports for the capital, Tokyo: New Tokyo International airport (Narita) and Tokyo (Haneda). Map **49.1** is a simplified map of the major air routes in Japan and the major airports.

▲ **49.1** *Japanese air routes*

1. Name the three Japanese airports that are linked to New Tokyo International.

2. If someone wishes to fly from Nagoya to Miyazaki at which airport might they change?

3. Can one fly from Nagasaki to Tokyo Haneda?

4. Which two airports are linked to Kushiro?

5. Naha is the main town of the Ryukyu islands. Name the Japanese mainland airports it is linked to.

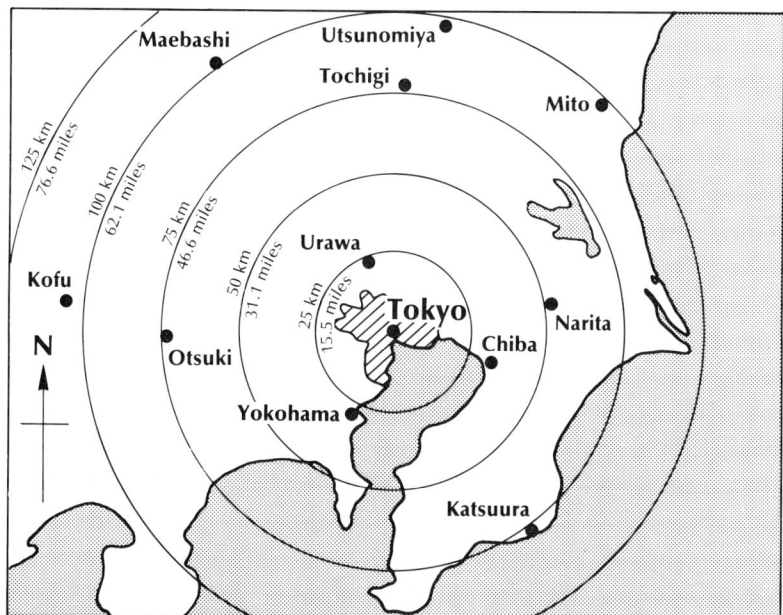

▲ 49.2 *Distances from Tokyo*

2 Map **49.2** is an isoline map showing distances in miles and kilometres from Tokyo to other Japanese towns and cities. Looking at the map, work out whether the following distances are correct:

1. Tochigi: 75km (46.6 miles) from Tokyo
2. Narita: 125km (77.6 miles) from Tokyo
3. Katsuura: 75km (46.6 miles) from Tokyo
4. Maebashi: 100km (62.1 miles) from Tokyo

Japan is now the wealthiest nation in the world. It has been very successful in selling consumer goods, such as cars, computers and videos, around the world.

Why is there such a demand for Japanese goods? Worksheet 49 looks at how important Japan's trade has become to the entire world.

Work this out . . .

The flight from Britain to Japan takes a long time, and crosses many countries. Find out from a travel brochure and an atlas:
a) how long the flight would take
b) how many countries you might fly across.

4. THE SOUTHERN CONTINENTS AND ASIA

50. GETTING AROUND:
Tourist Tokyo

Map **50.1** is from a Japanese tourist brochure. It shows the central part of Tokyo. Tourist maps usually have a great deal of information on them, and show the visitor all the places of interest. Look at the details of map **50.1** very carefully.

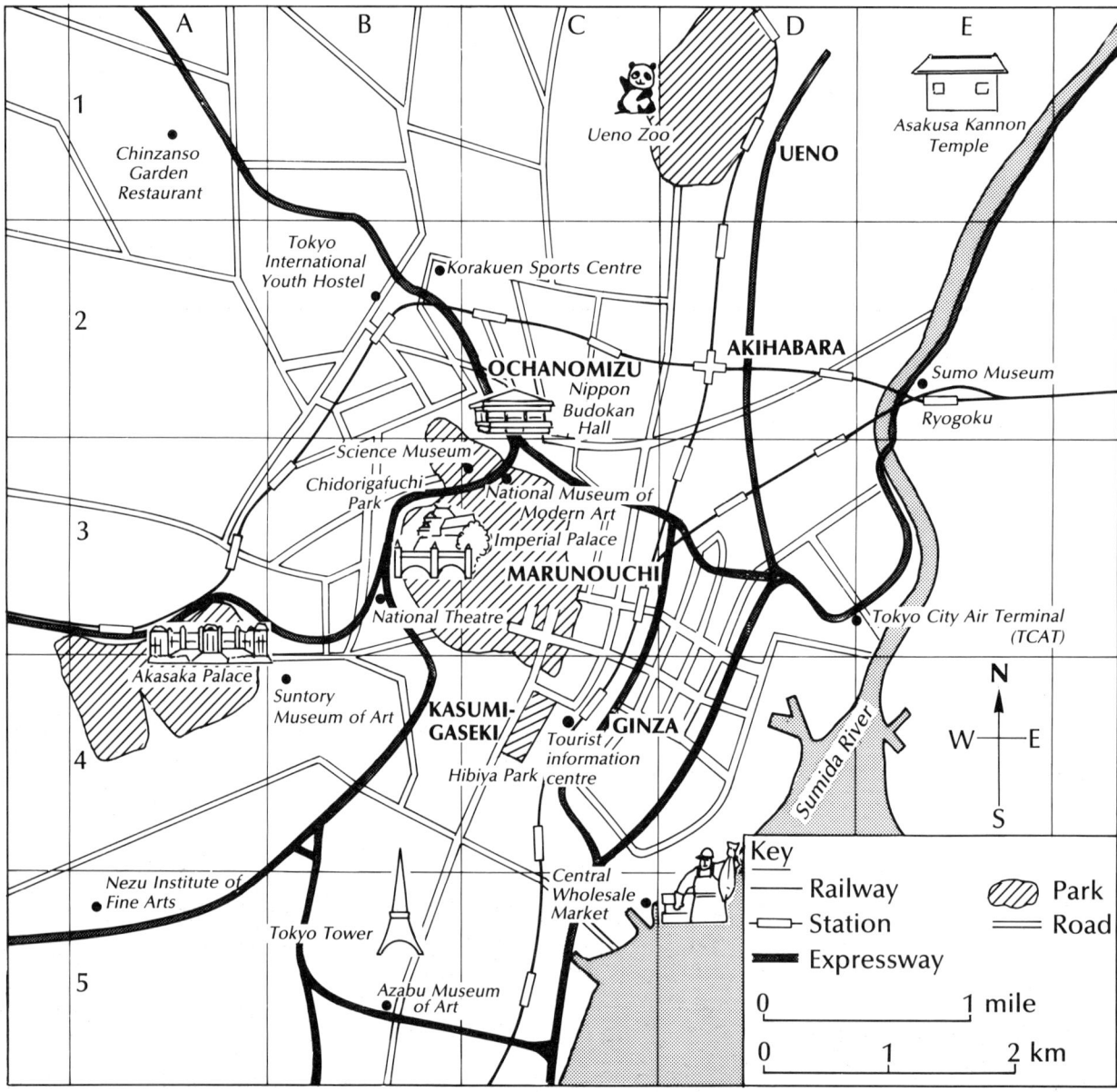

▲ 50.1 *Central Tokyo*

Harrison Junior arrives by internal Japanese flight at Tokyo City Air Terminal. He plans to stay at the Tokyo International Youth Hostel. His first stop is the Hibiya Park where he collects maps from the Tourist Information Centre. He takes the train to Tokyo's business centre, Marunouchi. He sees the outside of the Imperial Palace. Travelling north-west, he crosses the Chidorigafuchi Park, which is famous for its cherry blossom.

Art museums interest him particularly and he stops to consult the tourist map. He considers the Azabu Museum of Art, the Nezu Institute of Fine Arts and the Suntory Museum. He decides to go to the Museum of Modern Art. Nearby is the Ochanomizu district. Harrison Junior goes there and spends a long time looking at art books in the many second-hand book shops.

His next journey takes him eastwards to the Sumo Wrestling Museum at Ryogoku. He could not leave Tokyo without buying souvenirs from the famous shopping centre at Ginza, which he visits before finally going to the Youth Hostel.

▲ 50.2

1 An American student – Harrison Junior – visits Tokyo. Paragraph **50.2** is a description of his visit. List the places he visits. These have been underlined. Alongside each name write the grid square in which the place is found.

2 The student has had a very busy time in Tokyo. Look at map **50.1** and decide what other places look worth visiting if he had more time. Write your own timetable for a visit.

Tokyo, the capital of Japan, has very severe traffic problems. The area is very heavily populated. As there is so little space to spare, the roads, railway tracks and monorails are in some places stacked on top of one another.

The overcrowding of trains and public transport is one problem. The pollution created from cars is another. These are problems in many cities around the world, not only in Tokyo. What solutions do you think there might be to problems of overcrowding and pollution? Worksheet 33 investigates this issue.

105

4. THE SOUTHERN CONTINENTS AND ASIA

51. CAIRO TO CASABLANCA:
Locations in Africa

Africa is a continent of vast deserts, wide open grasslands, mysterious mountains, surf-fringed beaches and deep, dark tropical rainforests.

It is a continent of many countries and peoples. Some of the countries are young states. Until quite recently many were **colonies**, ruled by the countries of Western Europe such as Britain and France.

The history and past government of many places in Africa have left their mark on their languages and **currency** (money). You can see this in table 51.1.

Country	Main languages spoken (in addition to local languages)	Currency
Egypt	Arabic, French, English	Egyptian pound
Kenya	English, Swahili	Kenyan shilling
Morocco	Arabic, French, Berber	Moroccan dirham
South Africa	Afrikaans (Dutch), English, Xhosa and Zulu	Rand
Namibia	Afrikaans (Dutch), English, German	Rand
Tanzania	Kiswahili, English	Tanzanian shilling

▲ 51.1

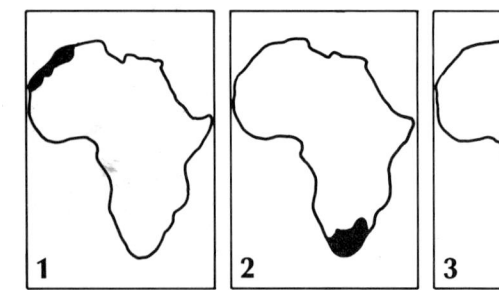 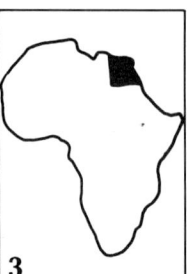 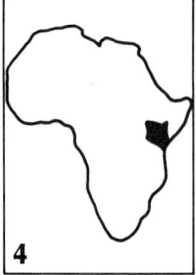 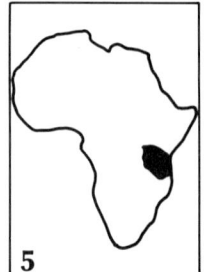 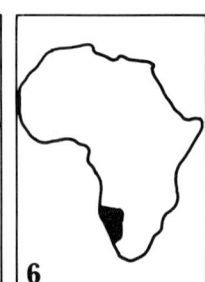

▲ 51.2

1 Using the maps in **51.2**, table **51.1** and an atlas, answer the following questions:

1. a) What is the name of country 5?
   b) What currency is used?

2. a) In what country is Berber spoken?
   b) What is the number of this country?

3. a) What is the name of country number 2?
   b) What currency is used?

4. a) What is the number of the country where Swahili is spoken?
   b) Name this country.

5. a) What is the name of country number 6?
   b) What languages are spoken?

6. a) In which country is the currency called a pound?
   b) What is the number of this country?

2 Many African countries are in a state of change. Some have new governments, whilst others are seeking new rights for some of their people. Some are at war. Several African countries have suffered badly from natural disasters and needed aid to help them. What else do you know about the countries in this unit?

Find out . . .

Many commodities are exported from Africa to countries such as Britain. Using an atlas, mark on your own map of Africa the countries and commodities from the list in table **51.3**. Then use an encyclopedia to find out how the commodities are used in Britain, e.g. tea from Kenya: leaves are dried and made into tea to drink.

Commodity	Country
Tobacco	Zimbabwe
Sisal	Tanzania
Uranium	Niger
Coffee	Kenya
Cocoa	Ghana
Dates	Egypt
Diamonds	South Africa
Groundnuts	Zaire
Cotton	Sudan
Palm oil	Nigeria
Millet	Chad
Copper	Zambia

▲ 51.3

4. THE SOUTHERN CONTINENTS AND ASIA

52. NORTH AND SOUTH:
Tourism in Africa

Many more people now visit Africa for a holiday than in the past. Here are mixed up travel descriptions and photos of six of the most popular destinations.

▲ A

1 This country has unspoilt beaches on shores lapped by both the Atlantic Ocean and the Indian Ocean. The climate is sunny and winters are mild. It is a very large country: it is nearly 1,000 miles from Johannesburg to Cape Town's famous Table Mountain. It is often in the news for its racial policies, called 'apartheid'.

▲ C

3 This country has a varied landscape with tropical forest near the coast, volcanic craters, lakes visited by flocks of flamingoes and the highest peak in Africa, Mount Kilimanjaro.

▲ B

2 This is a land of sand dunes and mountains. The Namib desert forms part of this country and the scenery is very spectacular. It ranges from deserts and rocky outcrops to deep gorges and dramatic coasts. The world's richest diamond mine is here.

▲ D

4 This country is at the edge of the Sahara Desert and contains the Atlas Mountains. Many of its towns have markets where the Berber people trade their sheep and goats and local products are sold.

▲ E

5 Africa's largest lake, Lake Victoria, is in the west of this country and the Indian Ocean in the east. The famous Tree Tops safari lodge can be visited and the country has many game reserves such as the Lake Nakuru National Park. The Masai Mara Game park is known for its herds of elephants and prides of lions.

1 Copy table **52.1**.

List the following countries in the left-hand column: Egypt, Kenya, Morocco, South Africa, Namibia, Tanzania.

Try to match up each country with one of the travel descriptions and one of the photos, putting your answers in table **52.1**.

Your turn . . .

You are a travel agent compiling a brochure to encourage people to take holidays in Africa. What maps and photographs would you use to attract customers? Make up some pages to go in your brochure.

▲ F

6 This is the home of ancient civilisations. The waters of the River Nile flow through the country to the delta on the shores of the Mediterranean Sea. The Nile water is used to irrigate the land. The pyramids stand in the hot desert and are visited by thousands of tourists every year.

Country	Description (number)	Photo (letter)

▲ 52.1

109

4. THE SOUTHERN CONTINENTS AND ASIA

53. WHOSE WATER?
African rivers

Map **53.1** shows some of the major rivers of Africa. They are used for the transport of goods and people, for tourism, for irrigation, and for **hydroelectric power**.

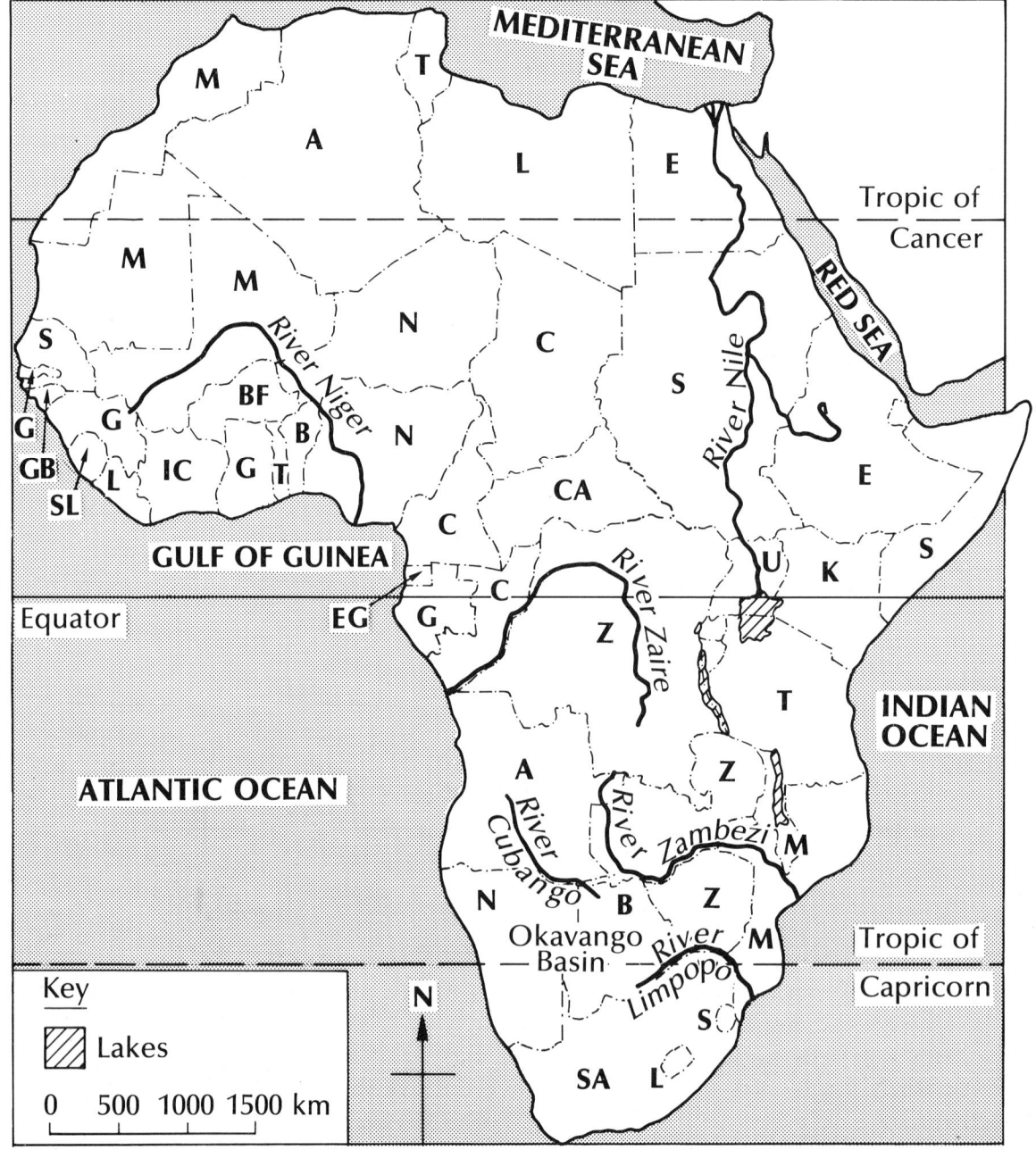

▲ 53.1 African rivers

1 1. Use the scale on map **53.1** and a piece of string to measure the following rivers:
   a) the Limpopo   c) the Niger
   b) the Nile   d) the Zambezi.
   Compare these with the Thames, which is 338 kilometres long.

   2. Which sea does each river flow into?

2 All the rivers on map **53.1** go through more than one country. This can cause problems over the use of the water. Use map **53.1** and an atlas to answer the following questions:

   1. Through how many countries does the River Niger flow?

   2. Using an atlas, find out the names of these countries. The initial letters are on the map.

   3. Can you think of a reason why the northern loop of the River Niger dries out for part of the year?

   4. If Ethiopia takes water from the Blue Nile, which countries, **downstream**, will find themselves with less water?

3 Some rivers form the boundaries of countries. This can cause problems over the ownership of the water.

   1. Which countries have the River Zambezi as a border?

   2. The River Limpopo is even more important as a border: which countries border this river?

The continent of Africa has a wealth of natural resources. It has oil, precious metals and minerals and fertile farming areas. But it also has its share of natural hazards – in particular **drought**. The northern half of the continent is dominated by the Sahara Desert – and this desert area is growing year by year. This process is called **desertification**.

Do you know any of the factors that make a desert grow? Worksheets 53A and 53B look into the way some African states are tackling the problem and action that needs to be taken on climate on an international scale.

4. THE SOUTHERN CONTINENTS AND ASIA

54. EAST TO WEST:
Time zones in the USSR

As you saw in Unit 38, countries to the east of 0 degrees longitude are ahead of Greenwich Mean Time and countries to the west are behind it.

Within large countries, such as the USA or the USSR, there may be several **time zones**. Sometimes the time zone boundaries do not follow lines of longitude exactly but follow a state or country border.

Travellers use an international time calculation chart to work out travel times when travelling through time zones. Business men and women who need to make phone calls to other parts of the world or send urgent telex or fax messages (see Unit 60), have to be aware of time differences.

Time Zone	Chief Towns	Difference from Greenwich Mean Time
1	Tallinn, Moscow, Riga, Kiev, Leningrad	+ 3 hours
2	Baku, Volgograd, Tbilisi	+ 4
3	Ashkhabad, Bukhara, Samarkand	+ 5
4	Alma Ata, Tashkent	+ 6
5	Novosibirsk	+ 7
6	Irkutsk	+ 8
7	Yakutsk	+ 9
8	Vladivostok	+ 10
9	Magadan	+ 11
10	Petropavlovsk-Kamchalskiy	+ 12

▲ 54.1 *ABC World Airways Time Calculation Chart: USSR*

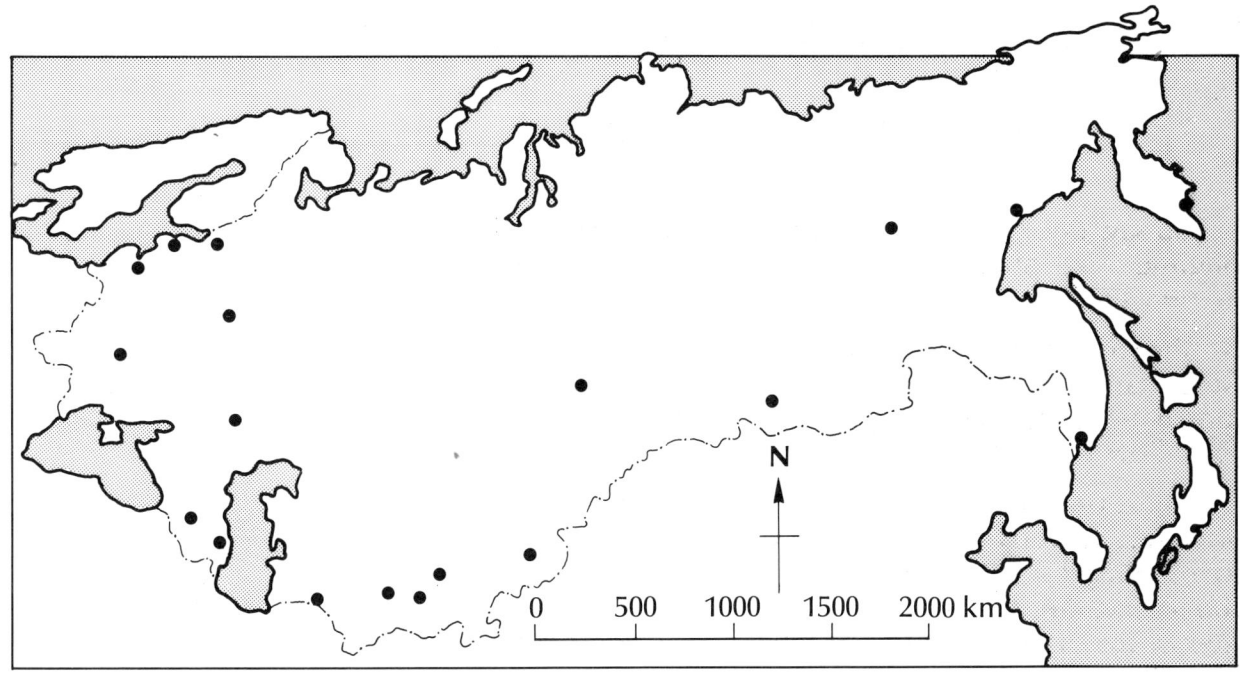

▲ 54.2 *The USSR*

1 Look at the ABC World Airways International Time Calculation Chart, table **54.1**. It shows the time differences between London and the major cities of the USSR. There is an eleventh time zone in the east. It covers the Chuckchi Peninsula, which is just across the Bering Sea from Alaska in the USA.

1. What is the difference in hours between London and Moscow?
2. What is the difference in hours between Tbilisi and Vladivostok?
3. What is the difference in hours between London and Irkutsk?
4. What is the difference in hours between London and Petropavlovsk?

2 1. On your own copy of map **54.2**, mark all the towns from table **54.1**. You will need an atlas.
2. Draw in the approximate positions of the time zones.

Sort out . . .

From an encyclopedia find out how Greenwich Mean Time and British Summer Time came into being.

5. THE WORLD

55. WHERE IN THE WORLD?
Continents and countries

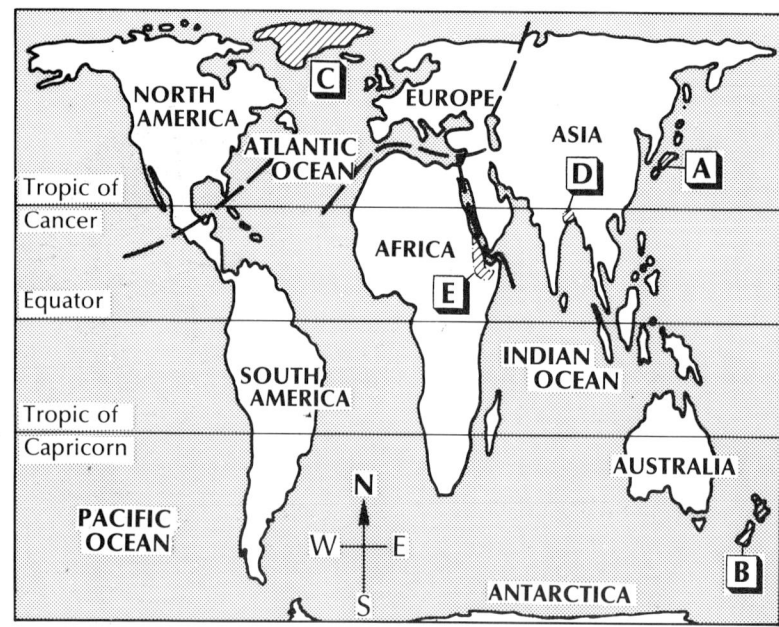

◀ 55.1 *The world: continents and oceans*

1 Map **55.1** shows seven continents, three oceans and three of the world's main lines of latitude: the two Tropics and the Equator. (The other two are the Arctic and Antarctic Circles.)

1. Copy the following sentences, filling in the names of the continents:
   a) The continents of _____ _____ and _____ _____ are west of the Atlantic Ocean.
   b) The Equator goes through the continents of _____ and _____ _____ .
   c) The Tropic of Capricorn goes through the continents of _____ _____ and _____ .

2. Areas north of the Equator are in the northern **hemisphere**. Areas south of the Equator are in the southern hemisphere.

   Copy and complete the following sentences:
   a) The continents _____ , _____ and _____ _____ are in the northern hemisphere.
   b) The only continents entirely in the southern hemisphere are _____ and _____ .

2 Map **55.1** also shows five shaded countries A–E. Use an atlas to name each country on your own copy of the map.
Now match the countries to these statements:

1. It is famous for producing cars, hi-fi equipment and videos. It has earthquakes.
2. It is covered with ice and snow most of the year, in spite of its name.
3. It has a monsoon climate, suffers from flooding rivers and from cyclones. It is one of the least economically developed countries.
4. It is a desert country which has suffered badly from drought in recent years.
5. It is famous for sheep, butter and cheese and a native bird called the kiwi.

Table **55.2** shows information about the population and area of each country.

You can see from this which countries have the biggest area and the largest number of people. It is usually more useful to know the **population density**, that is, the number of people in each square kilometre. It makes it easier to compare the countries.

To find this figure you divide the population by the area. For example, country A has a population of 117,600,000. Divide that by the area, 372,000 km². The density is just over 316 people per square kilometre.

	Population (millions)	Area (km²)
A	117.6	372,000
B	3.3	269,000
C	0.05	2,186,000
D	90.7	144,000
E	31.8	1,222,000

▲ 55.2

3 1. Copy table **55.2** and work out the figures for the other countries for yourself using a calculator.
2. Which are the least densely populated and the most densely populated countries?

More to do . . .

All these countries suffer from natural disasters but D and E have been most badly affected recently. Find out about these disasters and the causes of them. How do other countries, and organisations like Oxfam and Save the Children Fund, help in emergencies?

5. THE WORLD

56. FULL STEAM AHEAD:
World shipping

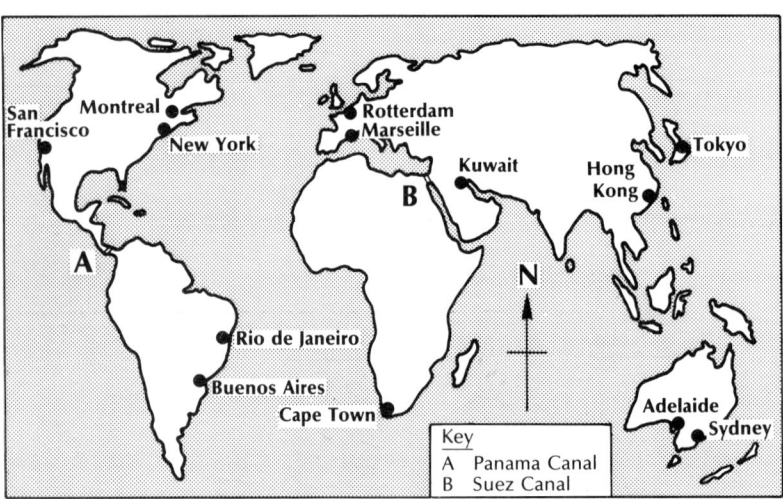

▲ 56.1 *The world: major ports*

1 You are a shipping agent with orders to move the goods in table **56.2**. You have only one ship available to do all the trading, which can only carry one product at a time. It is important that you travel the shortest possible distance and avoid travelling with an empty hold if possible.

1. Mark in London on your copy of map **56.1** and then draw in your route. You may use the Suez Canal (B) or Panama Canal (A) if you wish. Mark each stage of the journey with a different colour. Make a key to show what goods are being carried.

2. Make a list of the ports marked on the map that you have not visited on this trip.

3. By moving some of the following goods: Dutch butter, American wheat, French wine, Argentinian cotton, or other products, you might be able to avoid having an empty hold on some stages of your voyage. Fill in the suitable products on your map.

In fact, very few ships would carry only one product. Most cargoes are mixed and carried in containers to make it easier to load and unload. Only cargoes such as

Computers from Tokyo to Sydney

Wool from Adelaide to Marseille

Machinery from London to Kuwait

Paper from Montreal to New York

Corned beef from Rio de Janeiro to Rotterdam

▲ 56.2

coal, oil and wheat that are loaded directly into the hold, or into tanks, are carried on their own. Tankers are specially built just to carry oil.

2 In Britain we **import** a great deal of food.
1. Read through the hotel breakfast menu **56.3**. Make a list of foods that are not produced in Britain.
2. How about dinner? Which items in this menu would need to be imported?
You may have to look up the ingredients of some dishes in a cookery book.

▲ 56.3

5. THE WORLD

57. PORTS AND PRODUCTS:
World trade

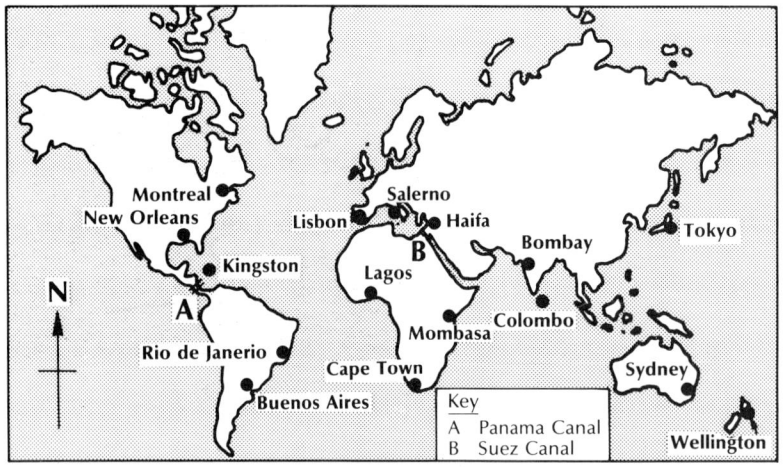

◀ 57.1 *The world: major ports*

1. A ship leaving the port of Wellington in New Zealand is loaded with frozen lamb for Liverpool, England. It calls in at other ports on the way. They are: Lagos, Nigeria; Sydney, Australia; Lisbon, Portugal; Cape Town, South Africa. The ship needs to call at the ports in the most sensible order, taking the shortest route. Mark the route on your own copy of map **57.1**.

2. A second cargo ship, carrying tea from Colombo, Sri Lanka, to Montreal in Canada, calls in at Buenos Aires, Argentina; New Orleans, USA; Mombasa, Kenya; and Rio de Janeiro, Brazil. What is the most sensible order for it to visit these places? Mark this route on your copy of map **57.1** using a different colour.

Not all world trade is legal! There is a secret trade in animals and animal products which is having a bad effect on some **endangered species** around the world. Britain has banned imports of ivory (which comes from elephant tusks) because so many elephants were being killed that the species could have become **extinct**.

Do you think the import of such goods should be banned? Worksheet 57 looks at this issue.

Table **57.2** shows ports, the countries they are in, and selected commodities (products) exported from those countries.

Port	Country	Commodity
Kingston	Jamaica	Sugar cane
Lagos	Nigeria	Cocoa
Tokyo	Japan	Televisions
Rio de Janiero	Brazil	Coffee
Haifa	Israel	Oranges
Salerno	Italy	Tomatoes
Bombay	India	Rice
Montreal	Canada	Wheat

▲ 57.2

▲ *The docks at Lagos*

2 All these commodities are needed in London. They have to be imported. Plan a voyage, or a series of voyages, to get these things to their destination. None of the products would take up more than a quarter of the space in the hold, so four cargoes can be picked up on the way to London. Remember that the ship must travel the shortest possible distance to keep down costs.

3 Look at table **57.2**. Jamaica, Nigeria and Brazil are all **developing** countries. A large part of their income comes from exporting agricultural products to developed countries such as the USA and European countries.

Consider why the following events could affect the income of any of these exporting countries:
a) a war
b) a disease affecting their crops
c) a reduction in **demand** (fewer people wanting to buy the product).

Home run . . .

Make a list of things in your home which have been made abroad. On a blank world map, plan a shipping route to collect some of these things from their country of origin and bring them to the British Isles.

119

5. THE WORLD

58. OIL FOR THE WORLD:
The oil trade

Table **58.1** shows some of the major importers and exporters of oil. The statistics show how much oil they imported or exported per day in 1987.

Imports (thousands of barrels/day)			Exports (thousands of barrels/day)	
USA	6,245	(2)	USA	745
Western Europe	7,905	(1)	Canada	630
Japan	4,125	(3)	South America	3,035
			Middle East	10,315
			North Africa	2,435
			West Africa	1,180
			South-east Asia	1,355
			USSR & Eastern Europe	2,910

▲ 58.1

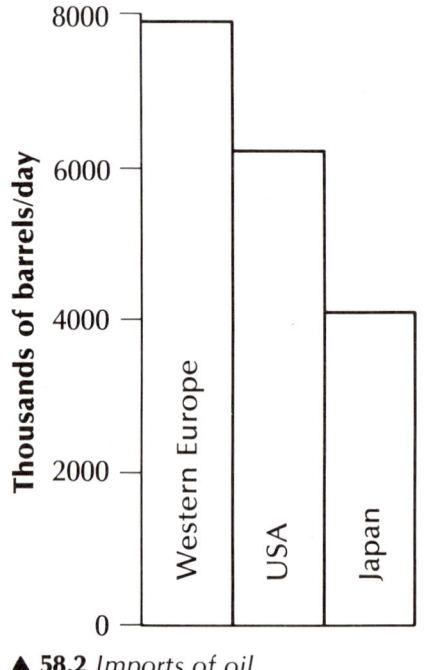

▲ **58.2** *Imports of oil*

1 The major importers have been ranked in order of importance. Graph **58.2** shows the same information in graph form.

1. Rank the oil exporters in order of importance. Then draw your own bar graph to show this information.
2. What do the statistics tell you about the oil trade? Write a paragraph to describe which areas of the world buy and sell most oil. Which country both buys and sells oil?

   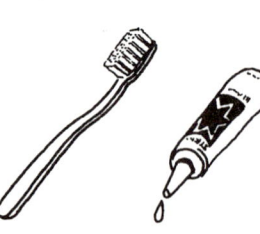  

RUBBER TYRE   DETERGENT   PAINT   CHEWING GUM   PLASTIC   GLUE   NAIL VARNISH

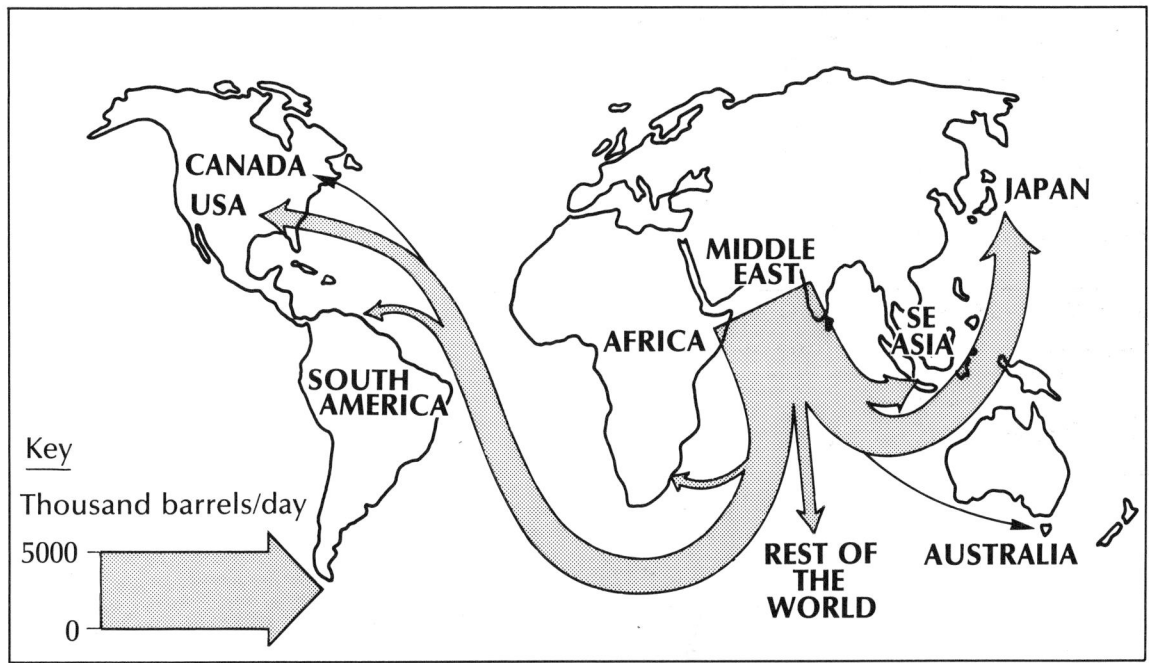

▲ **58.3** *Movement of Middle Eastern oil (excluding Western Europe)*

2 Western Europe is the Middle East's biggest customer. Map **58.3** has **flow lines** to show where the rest of the Middle Eastern oil exports go. The thickness of the lines shows how much is going to each area.

1. Use the figures in table **58.4** to draw similar flow lines to show the oil exports of the USA. Draw them on a blank world map. The scale will be different to map **58.3** because the United States exports much less oil than the Middle East. Use 10mm to represent 100,000 barrels per day.

Destination	Quantity (thousands of barrels/day)	% of USA oil exports
Canada	90	12
South America	298	40
Western Europe	186	25
South-east Asia	74	10
Japan	30	4
Australia	8.7	1
Other destinations	60	8
Total	746.7	100

◀ **58.4** *US oil exports*

5. THE WORLD

59. AROUND THE WORLD:
A world cruise

Cruising on a luxury liner is a popular but expensive holiday. The distances can be short, as on a Scandinavian or Mediterranean cruise, or much longer, for example, to South or North America. A long cruise would take several weeks, or even months, because ocean travel is so much slower than air travel.

				Southampton		
				Rio de Janeiro	5031	
			New York	4950	3118	
		Aden	6580	7601	4334	
	Alexandria	1540	5040	6061	2940	
Tunis	1040	2434	4000	5021	1930	
Bermuda 3591	4631	6171	1835	2907	2986	

◀ 59.1

Southampton to Rio de Janeiro 5031 nautical miles

Tunis to New York 4000 nautical miles

1 Table **59.1** shows a section of a shipping chart. The distances are in nautical miles, which are almost 4 feet (120 centimetres) shorter than an ordinary mile.

1. What is the shortest distance shown on the chart?
2. What is the longest distance shown?
3. How far is it in nautical miles from Southampton, Britain's main cruise port, to New York?
4. How far is it from Southampton to Bermuda?

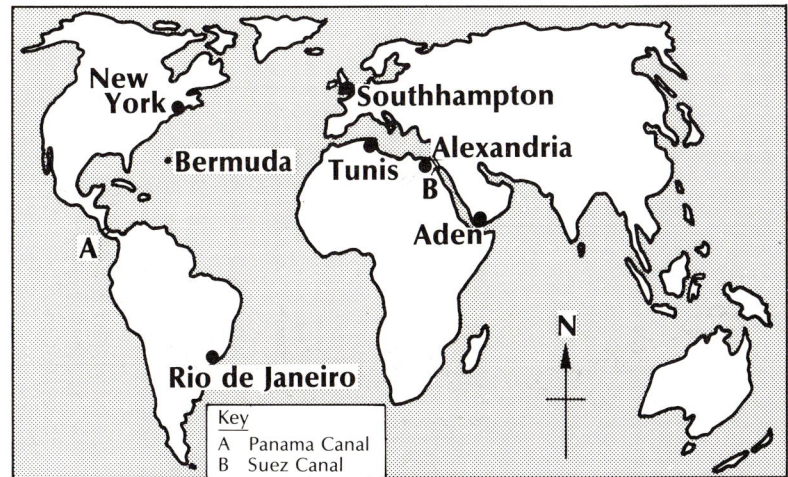

▲ **59.2** *The world: cruise destinations*

2 Look at the world map **59.2**.

1. In what direction would you travel if you cruised from Southampton to Bermuda?

2. In what direction would you travel from Southampton to Alexandria?

Time zones were explained in Units 38 and 54. Refer back to those units if necessary.

3. Would you have to put your watch forward or back going to Alexandria?

4. Which place on table **59.1** is the furthest ahead of Greenwich Mean Time?

5. If you were cruising from Aden to Rio de Janeiro it would be possible to go by two routes in two different directions, with very little difference in distance between them. Look at the map and work out what these routes are.

Now follow on . . .

Plan a long cruise visiting all the places shown on table **59.1**, without going back on your tracks. Write an itinerary for your journey. Find out what you could see in each place. Calculate how much time you might need to spend ashore. Then use Worksheet 59 to decide what health precautions might be needed for your visit to each place.

5. THE WORLD

60. POST EARLY FOR CHRISTMAS:
Postal zones

The Royal Mail has worked out how far in advance we in Britain need to post letters, parcels and cards in order to reach overseas destinations by Christmas. Diagram **60.1** shows some of these.

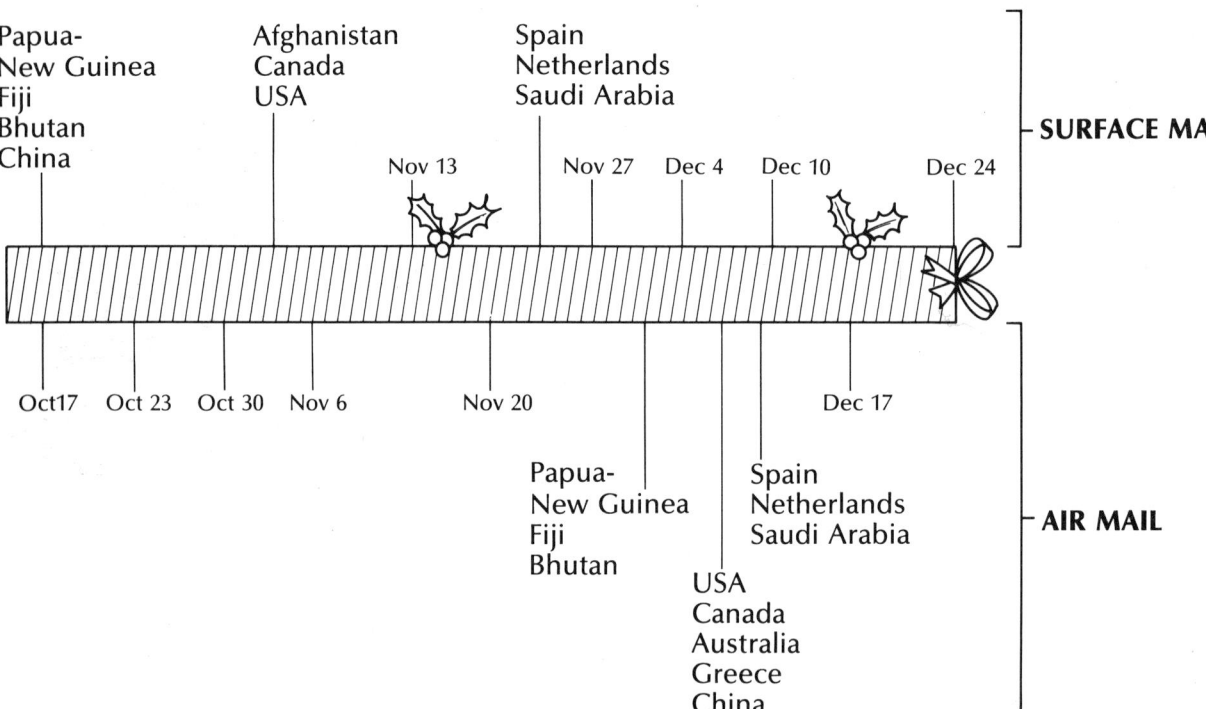

▼ 60.1

1
1. Air mail letters must be posted by 18 November to St Helena and by 24 October to the Pitcairn Islands. Copy diagram **60.1** and add the air mail posting dates for St Helena and the Pitcairn Islands.

2. Look in an atlas and find St Helena and the Pitcairn Islands. In which oceans are they located?

3. Why do you think letters have to be posted so early?

2
1. Look at the world map **60.2**, which shows seven shaded countries. Copy table **60.3** and fill in each column. Fill in the names of the countries using an atlas, and the posting dates using diagram **60.1**.

124

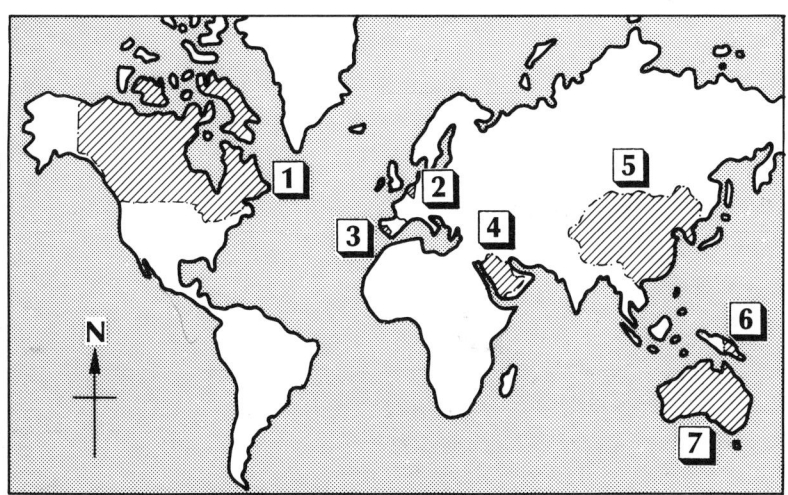

▲ **60.2** *The world*

Number of country	Name of country	Surface posting date	Air Mail posting date
1			
2			
3			
4			
5			
6			
7			

◀ 60.3

Electronic mail . . .

Some companies send messages via **electronic mail**. A person can type a message into a computer which can be sent to other computers on the same network almost instantly.

Information – including pictures – can also be sent using a **facsimile** or **fax** machine connected to telephone lines. Information is copied electronically and sent along telephone lines – anywhere in the world – to another machine. This converts the electronic message into an exact copy of the original information.

Do you know of other kinds of electronic mail? List some advantages and disadvantages of each kind of electronic communication.

5. THE WORLD

61. WORLD SEARCH:
A world quiz

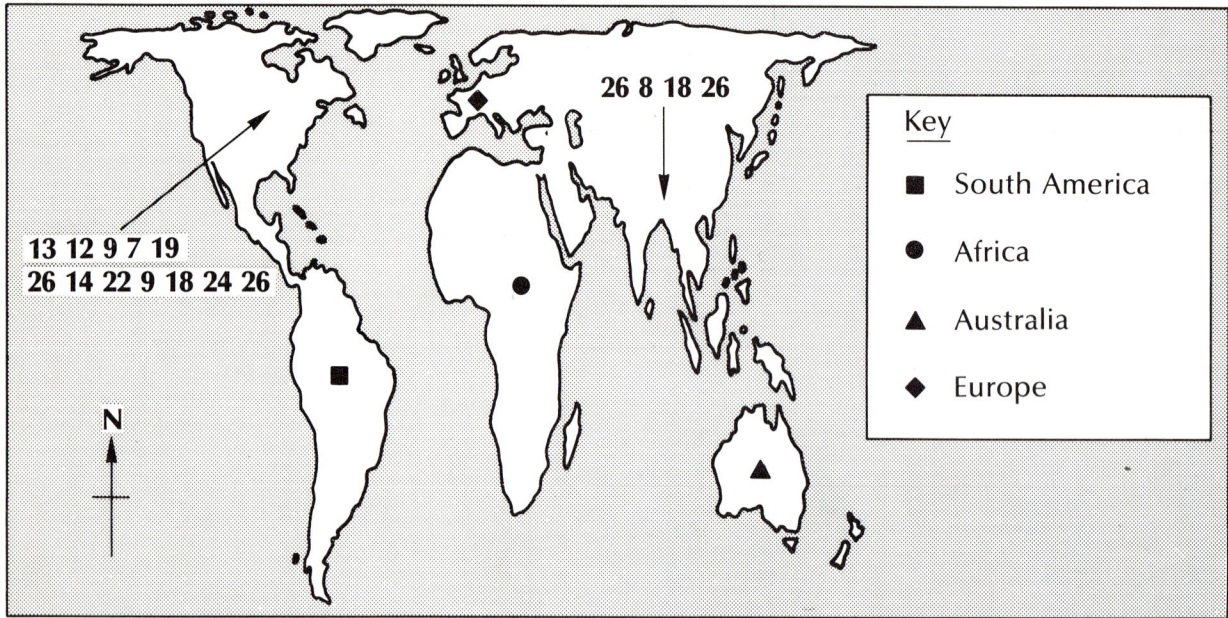

▲ 61.1 *Quiz map of the world*

Map **61.1** shows the names and locations of some of the continents of the world.

1
1. What are the names of the two continents given in number code on the map?

2. What is the name and location of the seventh continent?

3. Use the number codes from question 1 to crack the code. Then work out the number codes for the other five continents. Find them all in grid **61.2**.

2 Find two oceans and fourteen countries in word-search grid **61.3**. Look for answers up and down, across and diagonally, forwards and backwards.

Atlantic	Ethiopia	India	Pacific
Brazil	France	Japan	Peru
Canada	Germany	Kenya	Portugal
China	Greece	Norway	Spain

25	11	10	10	4	8	14	26	7
12	14	9	6	2	12	18	13	22
12	26	7	13	26	6	21	7	6
3	6	6	12	21	7	23	26	9
4	8	5	9	18	19	26	9	12
15	7	4	7	13	26	12	24	11
19	9	22	19	12	14	9	7	22
18	26	21	26	3	22	8	18	5
16	15	1	14	11	9	7	24	6
20	18	3	22	14	18	15	26	8
23	26	21	9	18	24	26	6	9
22	5	2	18	12	26	8	5	1
10	4	1	24	13	5	18	3	10
26	18	18	26	22	7	26	2	4

▲ 61.2

K	B	O	Z	V	A	E	J	T	R	W	A
I	E	K	S	C	H	I	N	A	D	O	P
L	F	N	P	A	R	T	Q	S	P	H	D
E	R	O	Y	N	J	P	U	D	A	A	E
T	A	T	L	A	N	T	I	C	C	A	N
O	N	C	S	D	E	R	N	X	I	J	S
H	C	D	M	A	Y	G	I	D	F	V	A
S	E	H	S	A	L	O	N	P	I	E	I
P	D	V	W	N	B	I	T	Y	C	L	P
A	J	R	E	A	Y	F	Z	N	R	Y	O
I	O	K	P	C	S	T	U	A	L	S	I
N	E	D	U	Q	I	B	E	M	R	D	H
P	O	R	T	U	G	A	L	R	N	B	T
X	E	L	H	D	R	F	Y	E	B	W	E
P	J	N	E	C	E	E	R	G	C	A	S

▲ 61.3

North or south? . . .

Make a list of twenty countries mentioned in Units 23 to 61. In one column write the name of the country and in the second column write down whether it is in the northern or southern hemisphere.

127

ACKNOWLEDGEMENTS

The authors and publishers are grateful to the following for permission to use copyright photographs:

pp 11, 13 (centre), 79, 85 (top right), Scotland in Focus; pp 10, 90 (bottom), Mike Read/Swift Picture Library; p 12 (top), Bernard Gérard/Hutchison Library; p 12 (centre), David Williams; p 13 (top), B & C Alexander; p 13 (bottom), Frank Gibson; pp 24 (both), 84 (centre left), 85 (centre left and centre right), 90 (centre and centre right), 91 (top left and top right), David Davies; p 28, JAS Photographic Ltd; p 38, Dr Peyto Slatter/Swift Picture Library; pp 50, 51, 56, 68 (both), 84 (top right, bottom right, bottom left), 85 (top left), Travel Photo International; p 64 (both), Sport Hotel Prem; p 85 (bottom right), Philip Wallick/Scotland in Focus; p 90 (top right), Keith Job/Hutchison; p 91 (centre left), R Ian Lloyd/Hutchison; p 91 (centre right), Michael Macintyre/Hutchison; pp 95, 108 (top left), 109 (left), 119, Hutchison Library; p 108 (top right), Gillian Craddock; p 108 (bottom right), Chris Johnson/Hutchison; p 108 (bottom left), Mike Mockler/Swift Picture Library; p 109 (right), P Moszynski/Hutchison

and to the following for permission to reproduce copyright material:

p 14, Granada Motorway Services Ltd; p 16 (map), Trainlines of Britain; p 17 (InterCity logo), British Railways Board; pp 18–19, road signs reproduced with permission of the Controller of Her Majesty's Stationery Office; p 28, Ordnance Survey; pp 32, 34, National Exhibition Centre; p 33, The Basketball League; p 38, The Associated Examining Board; p 40, Seven Sisters Country Park; p 43, Torbay Tourist Board; p 46, Tyne and Wear Passenger Transport Executive; p 47, London Regional Transport; p 78, John Lawson, The Sunday Times, 22 May 1988; p 112, ABC International.

Cover photograph by Chris Gilbert

Technical Artwork by Art Construction

Cartoons by Philip Page

Every effort has been made to contact copyright holders. We will be pleased to rectify any omissions in future printings.